# HOW
## *Baseball*
# BEGAN

From the

Baseball Library

of

Joe Giannatelli

**BABE RUTH**
P.—Boston Red Sox
151

# HOW *Baseball* BEGAN

## RON McCULLOCH

Warwick Publishing Inc.
Los Angeles    Toronto

ISBN 1-895629-44-6

Published by:
Warwick Publishing Inc., 24 Mercer Street, Toronto, Ontario M5V 1H3
Warwick Publishing Inc., 1300 N. Alexandria, Los Angeles, CA 90027

Distributed by:
Firefly Books Ltd., 250 Sparks Ave, Willowdale, Ontario M2H 2S4

Cover Design: Cary Hyodo
Text Design: Nick Pitt

Printed and bound in Canada by Best Book Manufacturers.

*For baseball fans everywhere.*
*The true owners of the game.*

# ABOUT THE AUTHOR

Ron McCulloch is a Toronto based television documentary producer, and baseball fan, who became fascinated with the early history of baseball while researching the subject for a television project – "As I discovered the incredible story of how baseball developed and evolved, I also discovered an even more incredible story of how the real origin of the game has been covered up for all these years… and how the one man who virtually invented the game has been almost forgotten. I wrote this book to put the whole subject into it's proper perspective."

*Below: The Chicago White Stockings were the pre-eminent team in the National League in the 1880's, winning the pennant five out of seven seasons between 1880 and 1886. In this mid-80's photo Manager "Cap" Anson is center, top row. Superstar "King" Kelly is second from right, top row.*

# CONTENTS

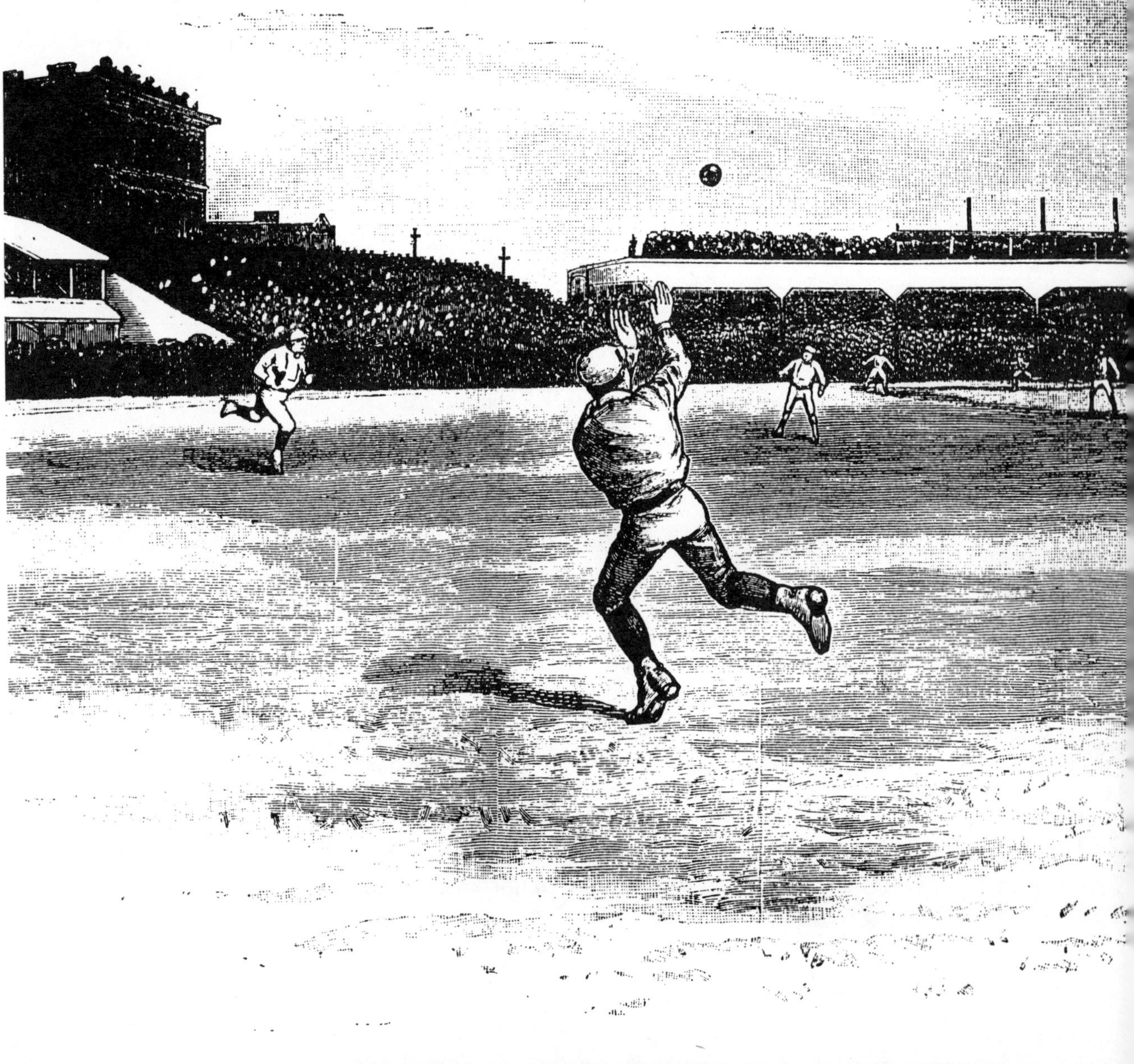

# ACKNOWLEDGEMENTS

Although I pored over many books and much reference material in researching this book, there were two books which served as my prime sources of information and I would like to single them out for credit. The first one is: the late Harold Peterson's superb biography of Alexander Cartwright Jr. "The Man Who Invented Baseball", which gave me great insight into Cartwright's life and achievements; and the second one is: Harold Seymour's "Baseball: The Early Years" which gave me an excellent overview of the first years of professional baseball.

Additionally, I would like to acknowledge all the help that I received from the friendly staff at the National Baseball Library in Cooperstown, where I did much of my research.

And I would also like to acknowledge the help and cooperation I received from both Stephen Speiser and Alexander Cartwright IV.

R.M.

# INTRODUCTION

If you're the typical baseball fan of today, there's a good chance you think that baseball began back somewhere in the early 1900s when men with names like Cy Young, Walter Johnson, Ty Cobb and Honus Wagner played the game. Actually, this period was only the beginning of the modern era of baseball. There was, in fact, a much earlier era of the game — an era that started in the mid 1700s, stretched all the way through the 1800s and ended in 1903 when the first modern day World Series was held — an era when baseball became baseball!

During this first 150 years, the sport evolved from a simple children's game where the fielders put out a runner by belting him with the ball as he ran from base to base, to become the great game we play today.

Unfortunately, today's baseball enthusiast seems to to know very little about this early period; very little of how the game originated (did some guy named Doubleday wander out into a cow pasture and just happen to invent it one day?); very little of how professional baseball began and who the first pros were . . . or very little of how our major leagues began and developed.

The purpose of *How Baseball Began* is to help fill in the enormous gap that exists in the average baseball lover's knowledge of this extremely important period in the development of the game.

You may wonder why such a gap exists. Well, in researching this project, first as a video production and then as a book, I discovered that the two entities that you would expect to have been making a point of informing us about the origin and early development of baseball — namely the National Baseball Hall of Fame in Cooperstown N.Y. and Major League Baseball (that muli-billion dollar organization that

*League Style*

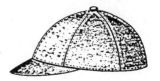

*Chicago Style*

*College Style*

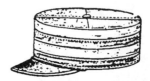

*Boston Style*

*Jockey Style*

*These drawings of early baseball caps and shoes come from an 1898 sporting goods advertisement.*

represents all of the major league clubs) — have been almost completely silent about the subject throughout the years and still are today. The reasons for this (the Hall of Fame's insistence on perpetuating the idiotic Doubleday myth, and Major League Baseball's attempt to curry favor with the Hall of Fame by keeping silent on the subject) are explored in chapter 5.

In any event, with the exception of "Baseball", the recent PBS television series by Ken Burns, the baseball fan of today has not been exposed to much information about the early history of the game. And unfortunately, the Burns series, as excellent as it was, tended to skip over a lot of important information on the early period, which is quite understandable because this is an era that spans some 150 years, and there is a lot of material to cover.

There has never been a shortage of knowledge available on the early history of baseball. Sources of information range from a few pages on the subject in most baseball encyclopedias to long scholarly books on the era — books that, unfortunately, most baseball fans have had neither the time or inclination to read. So, what we've attempted to do with this book is to bring this whole exciting and important era of early baseball alive through a combination of concise, knowledgeable text, a large collection of early photographs of the era, and an assortment of both early and original artwork.

A look at the early era of the game should be part of every baseball enthusiast's basic education, for how can anyone call themselves a true baseball fan without an understanding and appreciation of the people and events that gave us this great game?

An important part of baseball's heritage has been ignored for far too long . . . so turn the pages and take a journey through the first 150 years of baseball. It's about time you discovered... *How Baseball Began.*

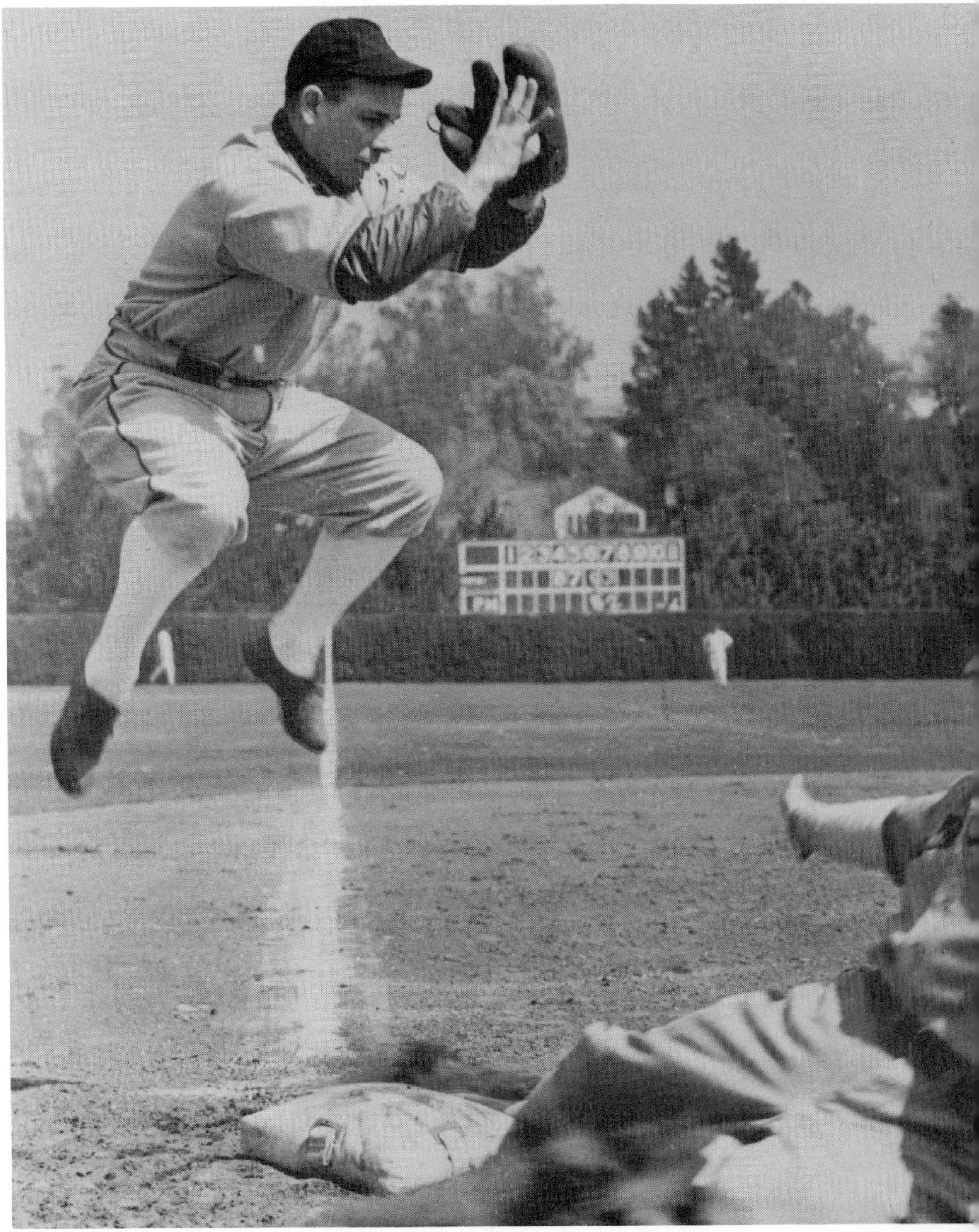

# CHAPTER 1

# THE MEANING OF BASEBALL

To many of us, baseball is more than just a game — it's a magical, spellbinding, almost religious experience, a wondrous force that takes over our lives when we're young, and stays with us for life.

It's not possible to imagine what North America would be like without baseball, for as our society evolved and grew, baseball evolved and grew right along with it, and became woven into the very fabric of our culture. And the effects of the game are everywhere: baseball jargon is part of our language; large sections of our daily newspapers are devoted to baseball news; millions of us sit in front of T.V. sets watching a single game; kids grow up collecting baseball cards and know the statistics on all of their favorite players; the ballpark is part of our neighborhood; and multi-million dollar baseball stadiums help to define our major cities.

Baseball is a game of vivid images. It's kids throwing a ball around in a vacant lot and it's 50,000 people jammed into a gigantic stadium cheering on their favorite team. It's home runs . . . double plays . . . arguments with the umpire . . . a glorious spectacle accompanied by the sound of balls popping in gloves and screaming hot dog vendors.

No other popular diversion has had quite the same impact on us as this game of ball and bat — a game that not only became a multi-billion dollar business in North America, but has taken on international proportions, with the pastime now an Olympic sport that's played in over 80 countries throughout the world.

Were you ever curious as to how it all started? Did you ever question how this simple game that became an event, and then a gigantic spectacle, ever got here in the first place? Did you ever wonder how baseball become baseball?

# IN THE BEGINNING . . . THERE WAS ROUNDERS

Baseball took root on this continent in the mid 1700's when English lads brought an offshoot of the game of cricket to our shores. This game, where the fielders put out a runner by belting him with the ball as he ran from one base to another, was called Rounders and it would evolve over the next 150 years to become what we now know as baseball.

*No one person* invented baseball, many people contributed to the development of the game, and yes, there was one man who contributed more than most, a man to whom we devote all of chapter two, but it was nevertheless a constant refinement of rules and regulations by many people over many years that gave us the game we have today.

Although the game of Rounders took on many forms, it usually involved a pitcher throwing a ball to a batter who would then hit it and run from base to base while the ball was being fielded. In order to get him out, the fielders would try to "soak" or "plug" the runner with the ball — that is hit him with it — while he was off base.

Even though rules for Rounders or Rounders-type games were occasionally published in books in the 1700s and early 1800s, the game was usually played according to local custom, meaning the number of players on a side, the number of bases (usually anywhere from two to five), the way they were laid out, the distance between them and

*The first known published description and illustrations of Rounders appeared in "A Little Pretty Pocketbook", a children's book published in 1744 in England and later reprinted in North America in 1762 and 1778.*

other rules would vary from place to place. Rounders was basically a pickup game that was *played by children*, with the rules constantly subject to change and friendly dispute.

For bases they used rocks, stakes, posts, inverted milking stools or anything else that was handy. Bats could be ax handles, rake handles, wagon spokes or any piece of wood, either flat or round, that was available. Balls were usually constructed by taking a piece of cork or some shreds of india rubber which were then wrapped in twine and covered with chamois or sheepskin.

In one variation of the game, there were no competing sides, you would just have the batter facing a yard full of

The *little* i Play.

STOOL-BALL.

THE *Ball* once ſtruck with Art and Care,
And drove impetuous through the Air
Swift round his Courſe the *Gameſter* flies,
Or his *Stool's* taken by Surprize.

RULE *of* LIFE.

Beſtow your Alms whene'er you ſee
An Object in Neceſſity.

The *little* k Play.

BASE-BALL.

THE *Ball* once ſtruck off,
Away flies the *Boy*
To the next deſtin'd Poſt,
And then Home with Joy.

MORAL.

Thus *Britons* for Lucre
Fly over the Main;
But, with Pleaſure tranſported,
Return back again.

TRAP.

PLAYING BALL

playmates. Another variation involved one player throwing the ball at a barn wall; it would then bounce off and another player who was stationed about 12 feet away would hit it with a stick and then try to run to the wall and back while the first player retrieved the ball and tried to belt the runner with it before he returned to his original position.

In addition to being called Rounders the game was also known as Round Ball, Sting Ball, Soak Ball, Burn Ball, Town Ball, the Massachusetts Game and sometimes even . . . Base Ball.

Another form of the game was called Catapult Ball or Cat Ball; in this game, a flat bat would be laid seesaw-fashion across a log or rock with the ball (or some type of

*This "Playing Ball" woodcut was originally published in the United States in 1820 in a book called "Children's Amusements".*

*Opposite top: This illustration from "The Book of Sports" published in 1834 shows rounders being played on the Boston Common.*

*Opposite bottom: Rounders was a game were the fielders put out a runner by belting him with the ball as he ran from base to base.*

projectile, often a piece of wood) set on the lower end. One player would catapult the projectile into the air for another player to hit with his hand or a stick. Runners would then go back and forth between bases while the projectile was being retrieved. Sometimes this game involved digging one or more holes in the ground, the batter would then have to stick the bat in a hole to attain safety from being put out. As a result, the game was sometimes called "One Hole Cat", "Two Hole Cat", "Three Hole Cat", etc. As with Rounders, there were no set or "official" regulations for Cat Ball; the rules would vary from location to location.

Versions of Rounders and Cat Ball were played in the 1700s and early 1800s on cow pastures, village greens and college campuses throughout New England and the northeastern states. Fortunately for us, this chaotic profusion of primitive ball and bat type games was about to come to an end, for the introduction of what would become a universal form of baseball was just around the corner.

*In the game of Cat Ball, a ball or some type of projectile was catapulted into the air and then hit. Runners would go back and forth between bases while the projectile was being retrieved.*

*Right: This is an advertisement from the 1885 edition of Spalding's Official Base-Ball Guide. The hats were apparently priced per dozen.*

# BASE BALL CAPS AND HATS.

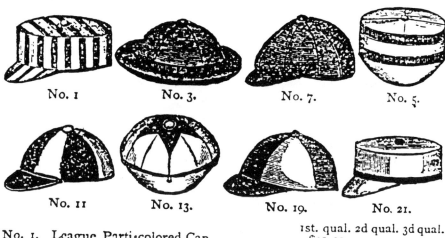

No. 1.    No. 3.    No. 7.    No. 5.

No. 11.    No. 13.    No. 19.    No. 21.

|  |  | 1st. qual. | 2d qual. | 3d qual. |
|---|---|---|---|---|
| No. 1. | League Parti-colored Cap | $12 00 | ..... | ..... |
| No. 3. | Base Ball Hat, any color | 18 00 | 15 00 | ..... |
| No. 5. | Base Ball Cap, Chicago style, any color, with or without stripes | 9 00 | ..... | ..... |
| No. 7. | Base Ball Cap, Boston shape, without star, any colors | 9 00 | 7 50 | 6 00 |
| No. 7. | Ditto, all white only | 9 00 | 7 50 | 6 00 |
| No. 11. | Base Ball Cap, Jockey shape, any color | 9 00 | 7 50 | 6 00 |
| No. 11. | Ditto, all white only | 9 00 | 7 50 | 6 00 |
| No. 13. | Base Ball Cap, Boston shape, with star | 9 00 | 7 50 | 6 00 |
| No. 19. | Base Ball Skull Cap, any color | 9 00 | 7 50 | 6 00 |
| No. 19. | Ditto, white only | 9 00 | 7 50 | 6 00 |
| No. 21. | College Base Ball Cap, any color | 9 00 | 7 50 | 6 00 |
| No. 21. | Ditto, white only | 9 00 | 7 50 | 6 00 |

Boys' Flannel Caps, per dozen ............................ $4 00
"       Cotton Caps, Red, White, or Blue ..................... 3 00

In addition to the styles above mentioned, we are prepared to make any style of Cap known, and will furnish at prices corresponding to above.

## BAT BAGS.

No. 0.  League Club Bat Bag, made of sole leather, with name outside, to hold two dozen bats. Each ............... $15 00

No. 1.  Canvas Bat Bag, leather ends, to hold two dozen bats ........ $5 00
No. 2.  Canvas Bat Bag, leather ends, to hold one dozen bats ........ 4 00
No. 01. Spalding's new design, individual, sole leather Bat Bag for two bats, as used by the players of the Chicago club..... each, 4 00
No. 02. Same size and style as above, made of strong canvas... "   1 50

## BASES.

No. 0.  League Club Bases, made of extra canvas, stuffed and quilted complete, with straps and spikes, without home plate....Per set of three $7 50

No. 1.  Canvas Bases, with straps and spikes, complete without home plate ........................ 5 00

Marble Home plate ..................... 3 00
Iron   "       "   ..................... 1 00

# A. G. SPALDING & BROS.,

108 Madison Street,            241 Broadway,
CHICAGO.                       NEW YORK.

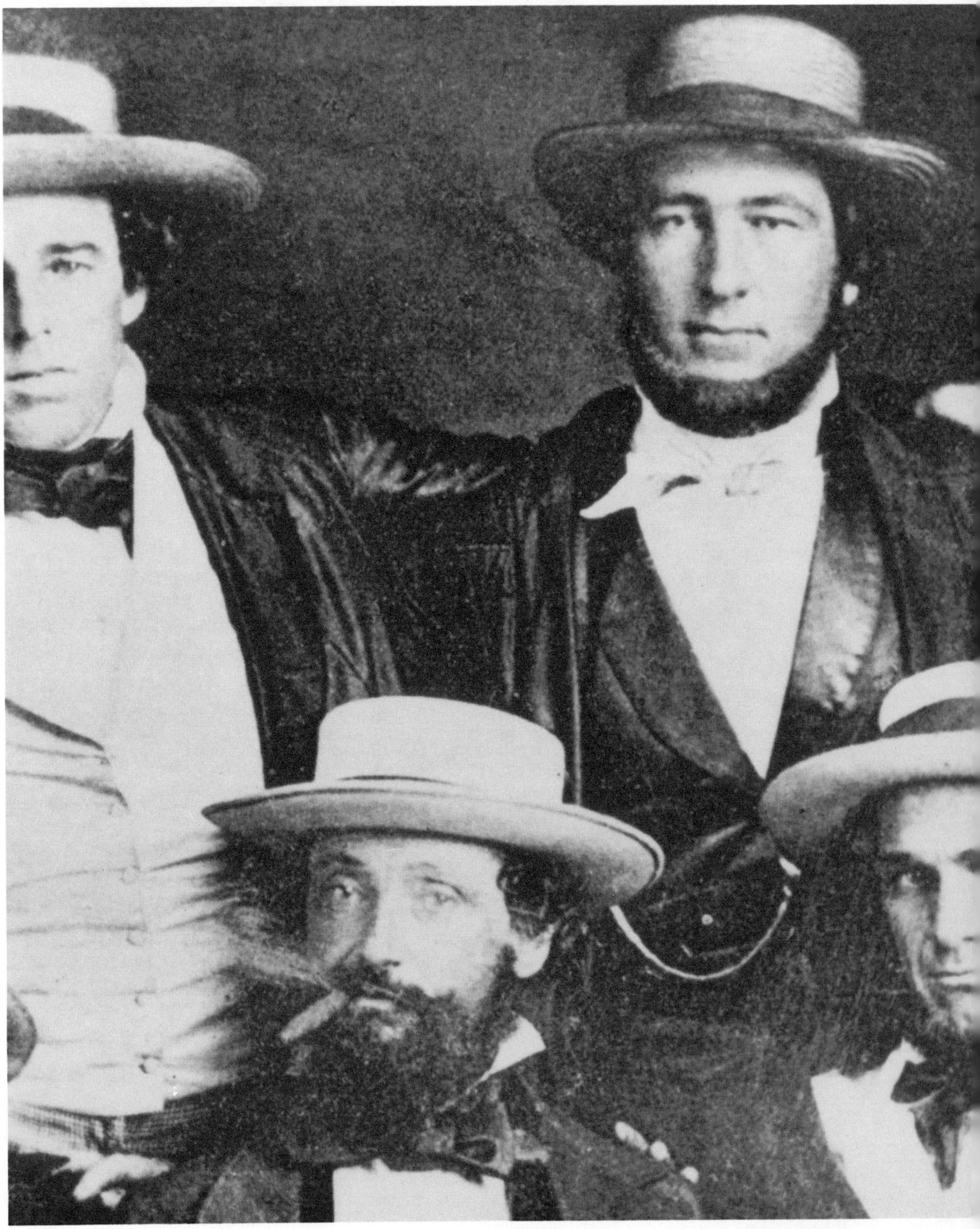

# CHAPTER 2

# BASEBALL GROWS UP

It was in the city of New York, in the year of 1845, that some of the most significant developments in the history of baseball were to take place — for it was at this time that a young fellow by the name of Alexander Cartwright put down on paper a set of rules and regulations that would be the foundation of today's game.

If anyone could be called the father of baseball, it is Alexander Joy Cartwright Jr. This 25-year-old bank teller and volunteer fireman, who stood 6'2" and weighed 215 pounds — which made him a giant in those days — was the founder of the Knickerbocker Base Ball Club of New York, a group of young gentlemen who usually got together on Sunday afternoons in the summer, in a vacant lot near the present corner of Lexington Avenue and 34th street, to play baseball according to Cartwright's rules and regulations. He'd show up each week with a new design for baseball and they'd play and experiment.

What Cartwright did was to take some of the various elements that were being used in the different forms of early baseball that were being played at that time, and integrate them into his game, adding a few wrinkles of his own along the way — and in doing so, Alexander Cartwright virtually handed us the game of baseball on a silver platter.

*A young Alexander Cartwright (top row, center) and several of the New York Knickerbockers pose for a photograph in the late 1840s. Cartwright's rules and regulations changed baseball from a simple children's game into a game that adults could play.*

*Left: Alexander Joy Cartwright Jr. - He was truly the Father of Baseball.*

*Right: How baseball was laid out before Cartwright changed it. The distance between first bound and second bound was approximately 60 feet, the distance between second and third was 45 feet, and from third to fourth, 60 feet. A base runner was out if hit by a ball thrown by one of the fielders or "scouts" . . . the batter was out if the ball was caught on the fly or first bounce. The idea was to move the runner from first bound to fourth bound which would score one "tally".*

He didn't care for the five-base layout that was commonly used in the New York City area at that time. Instead Cartwright incorporated a diamond configuration that was then popular in the Philadelphia vicinity, but he was not satisfied with the distance between the bases — he thought they were too close together — so, after a bit of experimenting, he placed them farther apart, specifying that the distance straight across from home to second base and from first to third base would be 42 paces. Now if you were to measure around Cartwright's diamond, you'd find that the distance from home to first, and from first to second, and so on, works out to be very close to the 90 foot

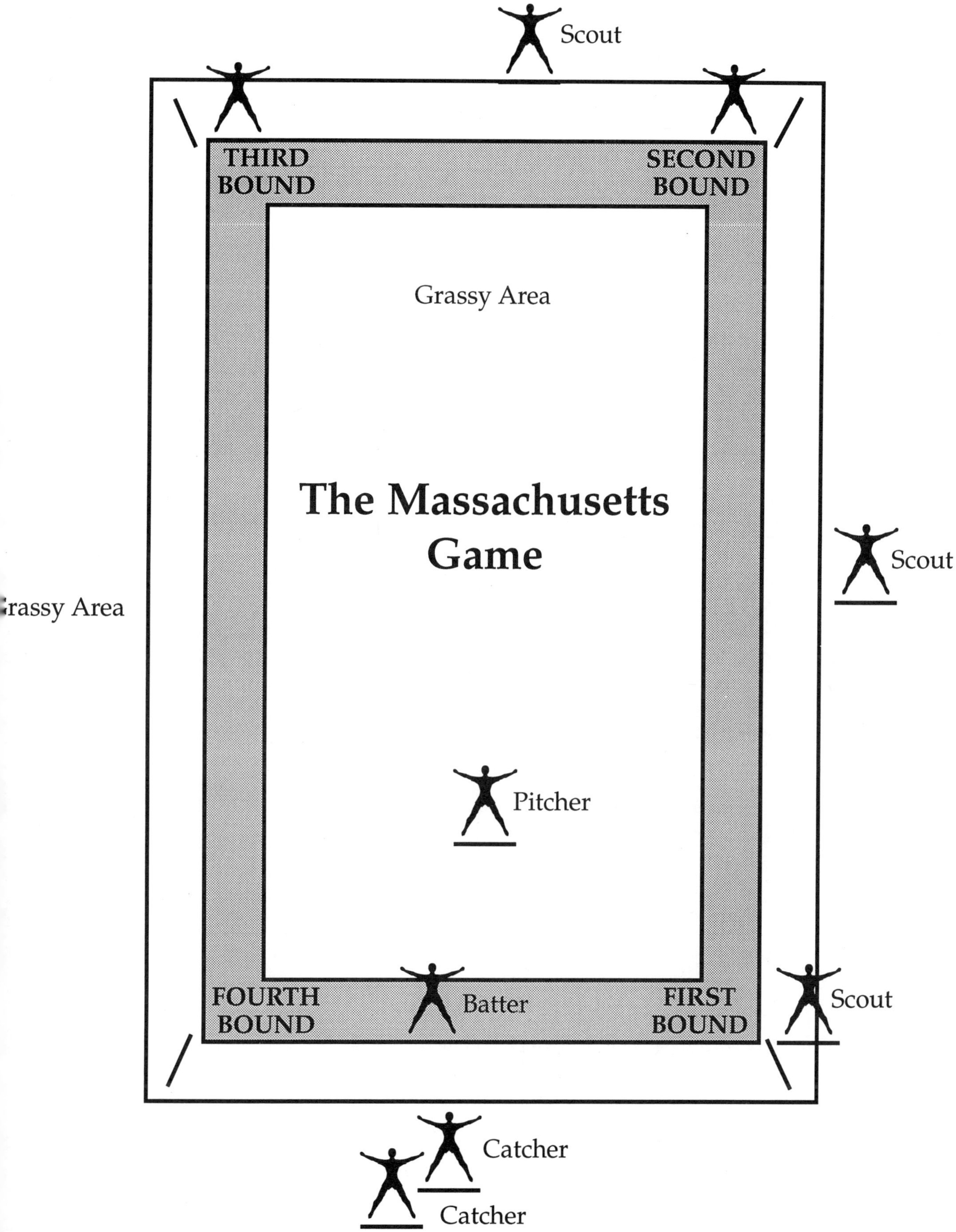
Scout
THIRD BOUND
SECOND BOUND
Grassy Area
The Massachusetts Game
Scout
rassy Area
Pitcher
FOURTH BOUND
Batter
FIRST BOUND
Scout
Catcher
Catcher

# Cartwright's Diamond - 1845

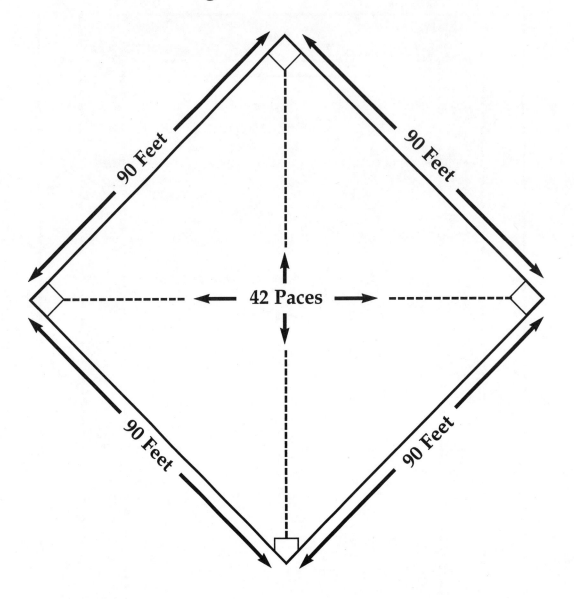

*The 42 paces that changed baseball forever*

*Cartwright preferred the diamond shape to the square five base layout. He modified the the size of the diamond to fit his specifications by walking off 42 paces from home to second, and 42 paces from first to third, thereby giving us the dimensions for the baseball diamond that we still use today.*

distance between the bases that we still use today. Among Cartwright's many baseball innovations, this one measurement was probably his greatest achievement . . . and, in retrospect, it was a work of pure genius!

Cartwright's concept of 90 feet between the bases meant that on a cleanly handled ground ball, both the throw and the runner would arrive at first base at the same time, with the throw usually beating the runner by a split second. This added elements of precision, perfection, drama and excitement to the game, because the ball had to be perfectly fielded and accurately thrown to get the runner out by half a step. If he had made the distance a few feet less, it would have given a tremendous advantage to the runner, and if he had made it a few feet more it would have given the infielders too much time to scoop up the ball and fire it to first.

And this measurement has stood the test of time. It has remained a constant part of baseball ever since 1845. Other dimensions have changed over the years — the distance the pitcher tosses the ball to home plate started out at 45 feet in Cartwright's day (they threw underhand by the way), then it was changed to 50 feet in 1881. Two years later pitchers were allowed to throw overhand and then the pitching distance was finally changed to the present 60 feet 6 inches in 1893. Outfield wall distances and configurations have always varied from ballpark to ballpark and still do today, but the 90 feet between bases has always been the same ever since Alexander Cartwright staked out his diamond in 1845.

But this wasn't Cartwright's only innovation — not by a long shot. Among the other rules and regulations he incorporated into his game were these:

- Tagging the runner: He did away with the practice of "soaking" or "plugging" the runners, that is throwing the ball at the runner to get an out. Cartwright replaced this with tagging the runner with the ball instead, or getting the ball to the base ahead of the runner.

- Canvas bases: He then eliminated the practice of using rocks or posts for bases and replaced them with flat bases. On Cartwright's first diamond the bases consisted of canvas bags filled with sand or sawdust and he used an iron plate for home base.

- The Shortstop: On his diamond, Cartwright stationed one player at each of the bases, and then decided there would be only one "short roving infielder" (there had been two up until then) and positioned him between second and third thereby creating the position of shortstop. In those days the number of players stationed in the outfield usually varied from

game to game, so Cartwright specified there would be three outfielders, and then he eliminated one of the two catchers they used behind the plate at the time, thus giving us the same nine positions on the field that we have today.

- Batting order: He also ruled that the players would bat in a regular order, which was to be decided upon before the game.

- Three outs: Cartwright decided there would be three outs per side per inning. Previously the whole team would have to come to bat before they changed sides, making for some extremely long ball games.

- Three strikes: Cartwright's rules also specified that a batter would be out after three strikes and that the ball would be considered foul if knocked outside of the 90 degree quadrant of the field.

- The third strike rule: Cartwright decided that a dropped third strike was to be considered a fair ball, thereby enabling the batter to make a run for first base (a rule that still exists today) and he decreed that a runner could take the next base when a balk was made by the pitcher. Cartwright also stipulated that a run scored before a third force-out did not count.

- His rules stipulated that the game would last until the first team had scored 21 runs (or aces as they were called then), after an equal number of players on both sides had come to bat. (The concept of the nine inning game did not come along until 1857).

Although some of Alexander Cartwright's innovations — such as the three strike rule and the actual diamond configuration itself — were not original ideas of his, what he had the good sense — indeed, the genius — to do was to take both original concepts of his and ideas he borrowed (and usually improved upon) from other forms of early baseball and blend them together to create a game of his own. It was a revolutionary new form of baseball . . . and it caught on immediately!

*Alexander Cartwright did away with the practice of throwing the ball at the runner to get an out and replaced this with tagging the runner instead, or getting the ball to the base ahead of him.*

# THE ORIGINAL RULES OF BASEBALL

As set down on paper by Alexander Cartwright, and adopted by the Knickerbocker Base Ball Club of New York on September 23, 1845. (Note - In parentheses, I have added explanations where necessary)

- The bases shall be from "home" to second base, 42 paces; from first to third base, 42 paces, equidistant.
- The game to consist of 21 counts, or aces (runs); but at the conclusion an equal number of hands (outs) must be played.
- The ball must be pitched (underhand), and not thrown (freehand), for the bat.
- A ball knocked out of the field, or outside of the range of first or third base, is foul.  (Note - if it hit inside but rolled out it was considered to be fair.)
- Three balls being struck at and missed and the last one caught, is a hand (player) out; if not caught is considered fair, and the striker bound to run.
- If a ball be struck, or tipped, and caught, either flying or on the first bound, it is a hand out.
- A player running the bases shall be out, if the ball is in the hands of an adversary on the base, or the runner is touched with it before he makes his base; it being understood, however, that in no instance is a ball to be thrown at him.
- A player running who shall prevent an adversary from catching or getting the ball before making his base, is a hand out.
- If two hands are already out, a player running home at the time a ball is struck cannot make an ace if the striker is thrown out.
- Three hands out, all out.
- Players must take their strike in regular turn.
- All disputes and differences relative to the game, to be decided by the Umpire, from which there is no appeal.
- No ace or base can be made on a foul strike.
- A runner cannot be put out in making one base, when a balk is made by the pitcher.
- But one base allowed when a ball bounds out of the field when struck.

# CARTWRIGHT GAVE BASEBALL
## *ADULTNESS*

Everyone loved this new game that Cartwright had come up with. Why? Well, what Alexander Cartwright, this 25-year-old intuitive genius, did, by introducing his rules and regulations, was to take, what had been up until that time, a simple children's amusement, and turn it into a game that grown ups could play.

As Cartwright biographer Harold Peterson so aptly puts it: Cartwright "introduced adultness and complexity

*This New York Knickerbocker game book from June 19, 1846 records the very first baseball game ever played between two organized teams under Alexander Cartwright's rules and regulations. The game was played at Elysian Fields in Hoboken, New Jersey. In the remarks column you'll note that Umpire Cartwright fined James Whyte Davis of the New York club half a York shilling (6 cts) for swearing.*

## KNICKERBOCKER BALL CLUB.

| FINES. | NAMES. | | HANDS OUT. | | RUNS. | | REMARKS. |
|---|---|---|---|---|---|---|---|
| | Tummy | 1 | | | | | |
| | Adams | 3 | | | | | |
| | Tucker | 2 | 3 | | | | |
| | Birney | | 1 | | 1 | | |
| | Avery | | | | | | |
| | C. Anthony | 2 | 1 | | | | |
| | D. Anthony | 3 | 2 | | | | |
| | Tryon | | 1 | 3 | | | |
| | Paulding | | 2 | | | | |

NEW-YORK, *June 19* 1846.                                      UMPIRE.

to a directionless kiddie pastime." His improvements made baseball "a game so different, so much more rational and interesting." Peterson came to the conclusion that this new game's appeal was basically due to its combination of complexity, logical reasoning and physical exhilaration.

Peterson also points out: "The standardized shape and dimensions of the playing field meant that teams could meet on equal terms wherever they played, as did the standardized rules."

In this radical new game that Alexander Cartwright and his friends played in 1845, there were several noticeable differences from today's game. For instance, they caught the ball barehanded — fortunately the ball was a lot lighter (and slightly larger) than the one we use today, and it contained a large core of india rubber which made it very bouncy. There were no called balls or strikes; the batter could just stand at home plate and wait all day if he had to, until he got a pitch he wanted to swing at, and a ball caught on the first bounce was considered an out.

It was called the Knickerbocker Game or the New York Game, and yes, it differed in several respects from what we now know as baseball. But nevertheless, it was definitely the basis for the game we play today.

Other groups of young gentlemen in the New York City area soon started playing this game Alexander Cartwright and his Knickerbockers had developed, and this lead to a monumental event that took place the following year.

# THE DAY BASEBALL WAS BORN

On June 19, 1846, just across the river from Manhattan, at Elysian Fields in Hoboken, New Jersey, the first baseball game ever played between two organized teams took place.

Alexander Cartwright's Knickerbocker club took on a team called the New York Nine. The game, which was played under Cartwright's rules, lasted four innings and Cartwright's team lost by the score of 23 to 1 — with Cartwright umpiring the game!

Many baseball historians point to this eventful day as *The Day Baseball Was Born*.

Young Alexander Cartwright and his Knickerbocker club had brought about a whole new era in baseball for, as we shall see in the next chapter, in the following two and a half decades the New York Game would replace all other forms of baseball that were being played in North America.

# THE FATHER OF BASEBALL — A MAN IGNORED BY HISTORY

*These guys were the original New York Knicks! A Knickerbocker team portrait from 1864.*

There can be no doubt that Alexander Joy Cartwright Jr. is the father of baseball. And furthermore, this young mastermind, who has long been overlooked by history, should be regarded as one of the great American innovators of all time, ranked up there with Edison, Bell and the Wright Brothers; for just as their creations became a major part of our lives, so did baseball.

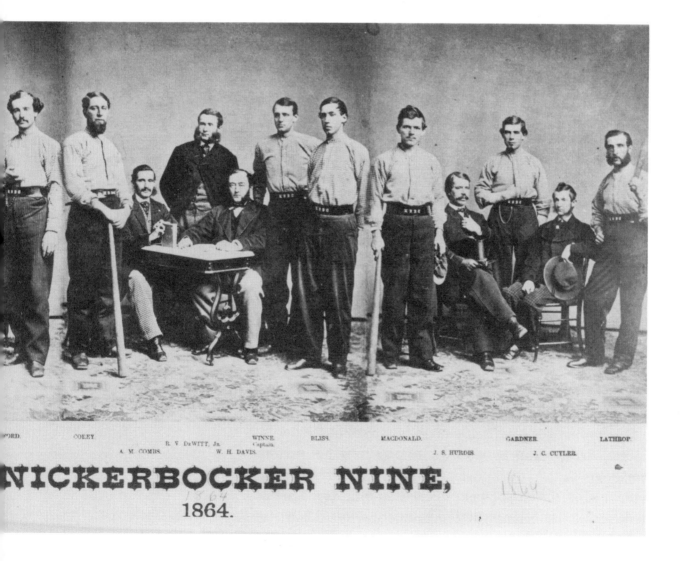

NICKERBOCKER NINE, 1864.

*Above: The New York Knickerbockers (left) and the Brooklyn Excelsiors (right) pose for a portrait in 1858. The gentleman in the middle with the top-hat was the umpire.*

Alexander Joy Cartwright Jr. was born on April 17, 1820 in New York City and was raised in the lower part of Manhattan Island, not far from the thriving South Street docks. He was the eldest of seven children born to Alexander Joy Cartwright Sr., a marine surveyor and former sea captain.

New York City of the 1820s and 30s was a great spot for the young Cartwright to grow up in. It was a New York that was remarkably different than the one we know today. The whole area was basically semi-rural, consisting of a series of villages and settlements connected together by country lanes. Stagecoaches would pass farm houses and meadows as they transported the local citizenry between such places as Greenwich Village and the villages of Yorkville, Kipsborough, Bloomingdale and far off Harlem.

*Overleaf: This is a Chromolithograph of the New York City/New Jersey Area from 1866. By the mid '60s rampant urbanization had drastically transformed the whole area from the semi-rural landscape of Alexander Cartwright's youth to a completely laid-out city. The population had increased to about half a million from the 175,000 or so genteel souls that inhabited the area when Cartwright was a lad in the 30's. If you look in the bottom left corner you can see a baseball game in progress at Elysian Fields.*

The riches of the world poured into the expanding, booming port and everyone in the region prospered as a result. It was a mellow, genteel, almost crime and unemployment-free place, and the New Yorkers of the time had a reputation of being honest, friendly and even polite.

As Alexander Cartwright grew up, he enjoyed playing the early forms of baseball with his young friends in the fields and meadows that abounded near his home. He also had a fascination with firefighters and fire-fighting. As a lad he hung around his local fire house and when he became an adult he became a volunteer fireman (and later on in life even a fire chief). He named his Knickerbocker Base Ball Club after the Knickerbocker Engine Co., a local fire fighting unit that he was quite fond of.

Alexander Cartwright could be described as a large, robust, outgoing, friendly man who was also extremely modest (this failure to toot his own horn is, as we shall see later, a contributing reason as to why he was almost overlooked by history).

Cartwright founded the Knickerbocker Base Ball Club on September 23, 1845. The club consisted of lawyers, merchants, Wall Street brokers and other young gentlemen of Cartwright's acquaintance — men with names such as William Tucker, Duncan Curry, William Wheaton and James Moncrieff, prominent young New Yorkers of the day, who got together usually once a week to play baseball for fun, comradeship and recreation.

Although Cartwright was only with the Knickerbockers for its first four years of existence, the club itself lasted until sometime in the 1870s, when it finally died out. (And with it, its great legacy also died out, another contributing factor to why the story of Alexander Cartwright was lost to history for many years.)

The Knickerbocker Club always maintained that baseball was a gentleman's game, to be played by amateurs, and in its latter years the club resisted offers to turn professional. If they had, who knows? The club may have survived, and even gone on to become one of the profes-

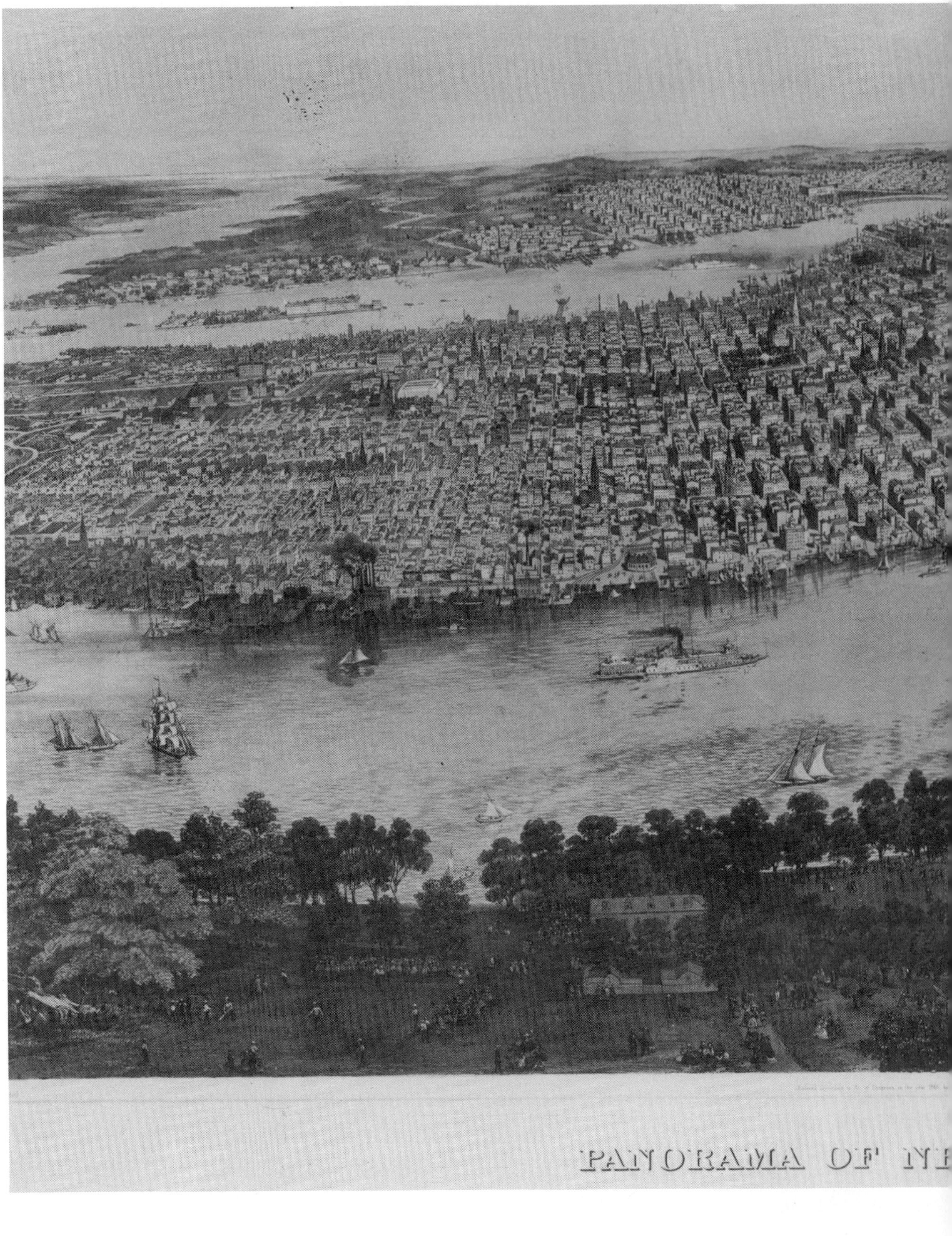
PANORAMA OF NE

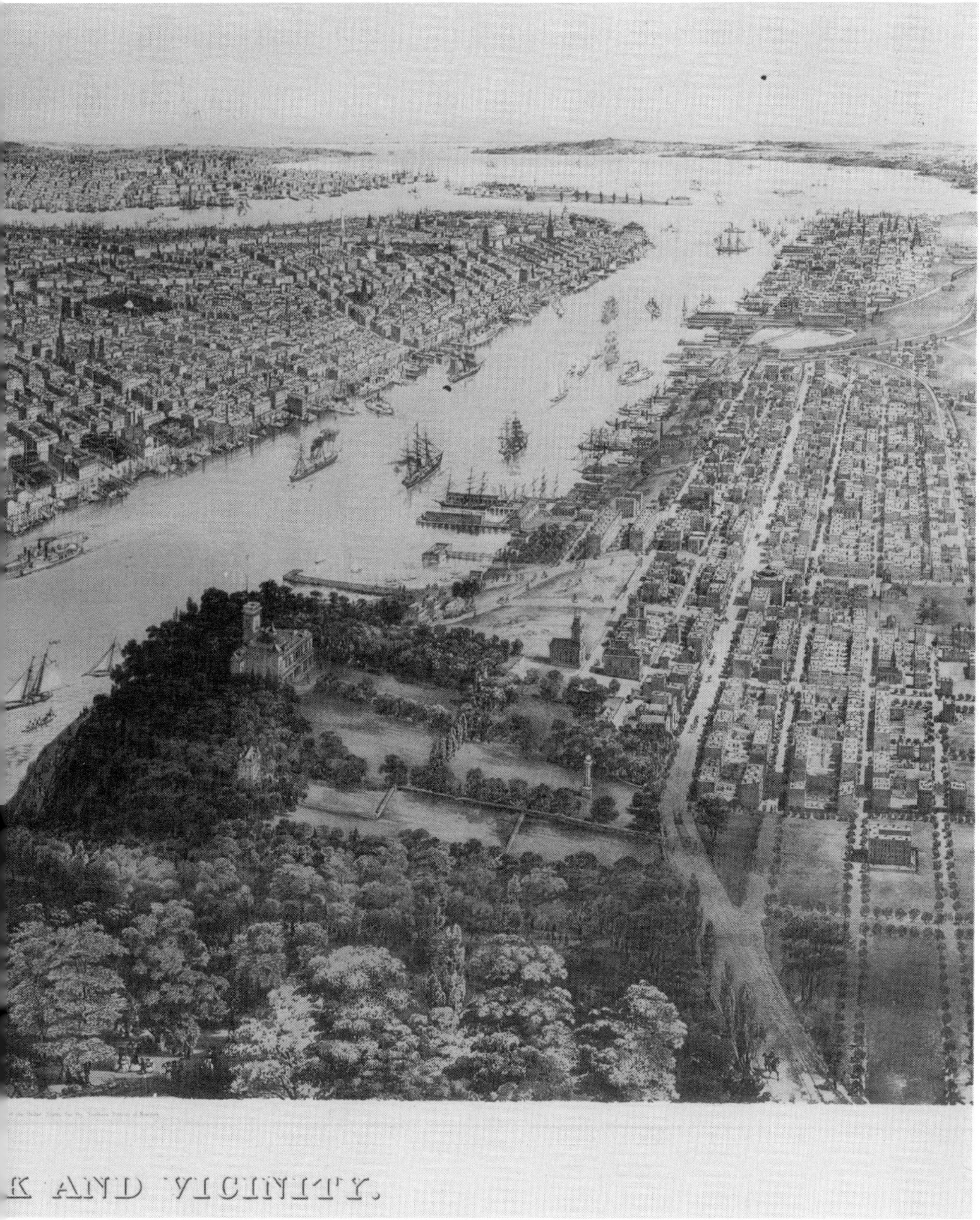
K AND VICINITY.

THE AMERICAN NATIONAL GAME OF B.
GRAND MATCH FOR THE CHAMPIONSHIP AT THE ELYSIAN FIELDS, HOBOKEN, N. J.

sional major league clubs of today, just as other amateur clubs did.

It is amazing that one man could have single-handedly contributed so much to the game of baseball, as did Alexander Cartwright, and even more amazing that he could have been forgotten for all these years, and even now, is almost completely unknown to the average baseball fan.

In Chapter 5 of this book you'll find out why Cartwright was overlooked for so long, and how he was finally discovered. You'll learn how an incredible fiasco, orchestrated by another great pioneer of baseball by the name of Al Spalding, almost buried Cartwright forever, as Spalding tried to create his own history of the game . . . and how the myth that he engineered was finally shot down by a letter from Alexander Cartwright's grandson.

But for now — with baseball having just been born — let's, in the next two chapters, take a journey through its infancy, childhood and adolescence.

*The Day Baseball Was Born. The first baseball game between two organized teams played under Alexander Cartwright's rules and regulations took place at Elysian Fields in Hoboken New Jersey, June 19, 1846.*
*NOTE - This Currier and Ives lithograph is not of that particular game, but of a game played at Elysian Fields in the late 1840's and can be considered a close representation of what that first game looked like.*

# CHAPTER 3

# THE NEW GAME CATCHES ON

In the first few years following that monumental summer of 1846, when baseball was introduced to the world at Elysian Fields in Hoboken, New Jersey, this new game of Alexander Cartwright's was mainly confined to the New York-New Jersey area.

The Knickerbockers themselves continued to play at Elysian Fields, as rampant urbanization had made it difficult for them to find a suitable playing field in Manhattan. Other groups of young men soon formed baseball clubs for both social comradery, and to challenge the Knickerbockers at their own game. The most prominent of these were the Gotham Club of New York, which was formed in 1850 (originally called the Washington Club), followed in 1854 by the Eagle and Empire Clubs, also of New York, and the Excelsior Club of Brooklyn.

Three more important Brooklyn clubs soon came along, the Putnam Club was formed in 1855, and the Eckfords and the Atlantics were established in 1856. (The latter two were workingmen's clubs, in contrast to the previous clubs which were composed of mid- to upper-class gentlemen.) In the meantime, dozens of lesser, more casual baseball teams had come into existence, as baseball mania began to sweep the New York area.

Bakers, laborers, clerks, mechanics and men from all walks of life had caught baseball fever and by the mid- to late-1850s more than a hundred baseball clubs flourished in and around New York City, as it seemed like every male in the vicinity had started to play the game, and hundreds of spectators lined the foul lines to watch them.

By 1857 the game had traveled far beyond the confines of New York City and had emerged in a scattered pattern

*A game of baseball being played in the 1850's.*

in various locations all over the continent — spread there with the help of America's new and ever expanding railroad network, and accounts of the game in such early newspapers as the New York *Clipper* and *Porter's Spirit of the Times*.

In New York state, places like Buffalo, Syracuse, Albany, and Troy all had local teams in the mid- to late-1850s, and the New York Game soon slipped across the Canadian border, as both Toronto and Hamilton, Ontario had baseball clubs as early as 1859.

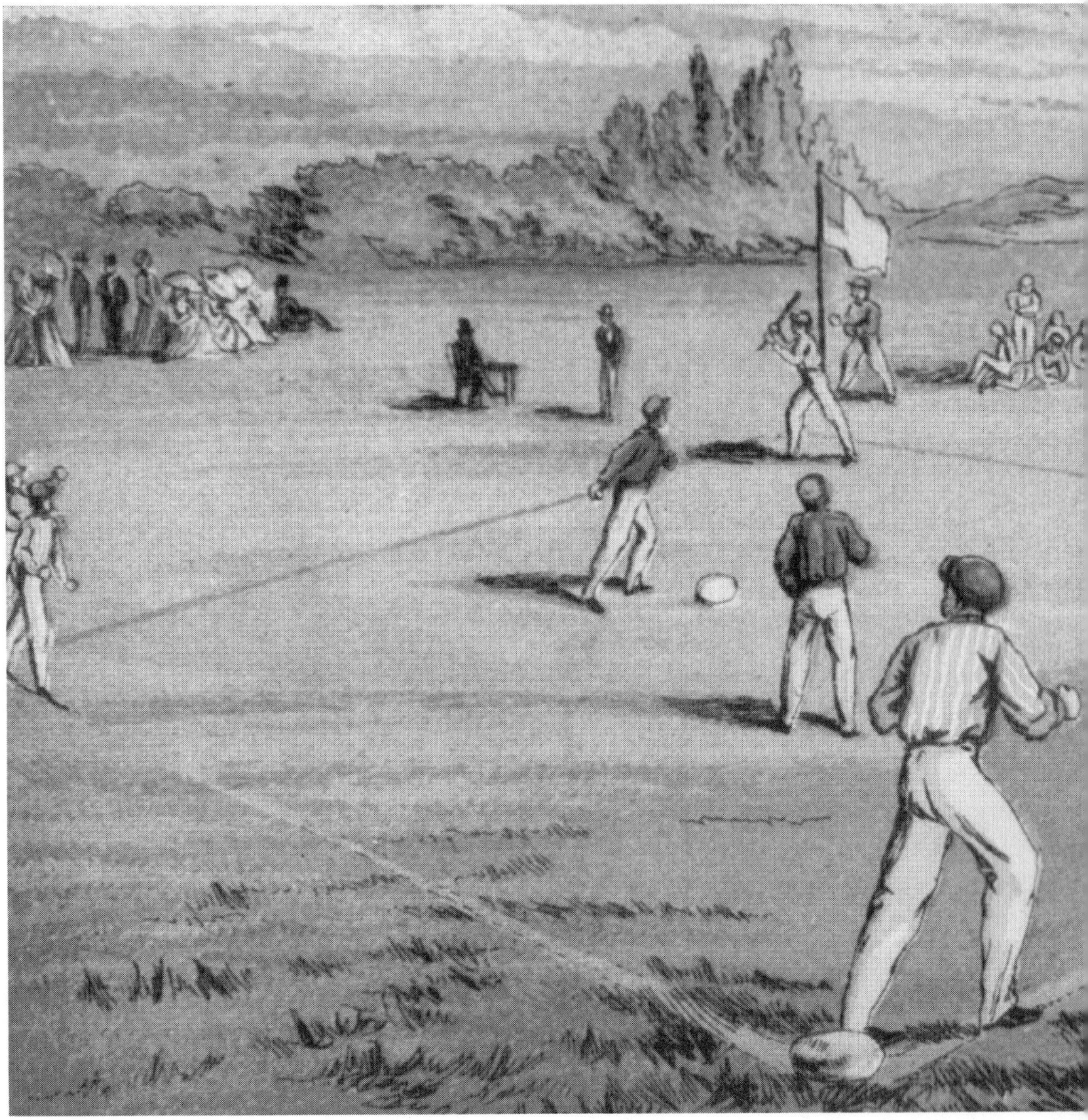

The first known team to play the New York Game in New England was the Tri-Mountain Club of Boston in 1857. Also in 1857, the Minerva Club was formed in Philadelphia to play the New York game in that city. In the next few years, they were joined by the Winona, United and Benedict clubs, and then in 1860 a group of Philadelphia lawyers and merchants formed the Athletic Base Ball Club, which is the predecessor of the very same A's that now play for Oakland in the American League.

In Detroit, the Franklin Club was organized to play baseball in 1857 and, that same year, there were reports of baseball clubs springing up in Cleveland, Chicago and even in the Minnesota Territory.

On the west coast, a baseball club called the Eagles (named after the New York Eagles) was formed in San Francisco in 1859. Baseball had been introduced there by two emigrants from New York: Alfred DeForest Cartwright (Alexander's Brother) and Frank Turk, a former Knickerbocker. And, as we shall see later in Chapter 6, baseball was even flourishing in Hawaii in the 1850s, brought there by the master himself, Alexander Cartwright.

In Washington D.C., two baseball teams composed mainly of government clerks, the Potamic Club and the Nationals, practiced and played each other in the backyard of the White House in 1859. And that same year, there were reports of this new form of baseball being played as far south as New Orleans.

So, in the first 10 to 15 years after its inception, the Knickerbocker game had not only taken New York City by storm, but it was also being played in scattered regions all over the country — and in another 10 years, total saturation would be achieved!

# TAKE ME OUT TO AN EARLY BALL GAME

If you were to attend a baseball game in the 1850s, you would find a crude but recognizable form of today's game.

There were no grandstands (and no admission fee); you would either stand and watch the game from along the sidelines or park your horse and carriage in the outfield and observe from there (there were no outfield walls). Sometimes a tent or pavilion would be erected for the ladies, to shield them from the hot sun.

*A drawing of a baseball game being played at Elysian Fields in the 1850's. Note the umpire sitting in a chair on the first base side (as there were no called balls and strikes, there was no need for him to be located directly behind the plate).*

A BASE-BALL MATCH

The field was all grass except for worn paths between the bases and down the pitching alley. There was no pitchers mound; instead there would either be a plate or a white line located 45 feet from home plate from where the pitcher would deliver the ball. He threw underhanded and the "striker" or batter who was armed with a bat of unlimited length (but could be no more than two and a half inches in diameter at its thickest part) could wait until just the right pitch before he swung, as there were no called balls or strikes.

None of the players wore gloves, the basemen seldom moved very far from their bases (and never covered a base

AN FIELDS, HOBOKEN

## BASE-BALL.

other than their own) and the catcher, who wore no protective gear, was often positioned some 30 feet behind the plate in order to catch the ball on the first bounce; only when there were runners on base would he come up and position himself directly behind the plate.

There was no players bench, dugout or bat rack. The team that was at bat usually stood or sprawled alongside the base lines with their collection of bats strewn about on the ground.

Technically there were three umpires at each contest, but only one was actually in charge of the game. He usually wore a frock coat and top hat and either stood or was seated on the first base side. The other two "umpires" were really not umpires at all, but advocates representing each team. They would sit next to each other along the sidelines, at a scorers desk or table, and yell "Out" or "Not Out" on close plays, in an attempt to influence the real umpire. The uselessness of these two "umpires" became apparent and they were eliminated from the game in 1858.

The crowd was generally quiet and mannerly — instead of cheering or boos, you would usually hear only polite applause and an occasional "Well done" when a particularly good play was made.

How did the players dress? Well, the Knickerbockers had set the standard for baseball uniforms and all the

*Early publications such as this 1862 edition of Beadle's Base-Ball Player helped to popularize the game throughout the land. You'll note that it was edited by Henry Chadwick, he was an important baseball pioneer who we'll learn more about in Chapter 5.*

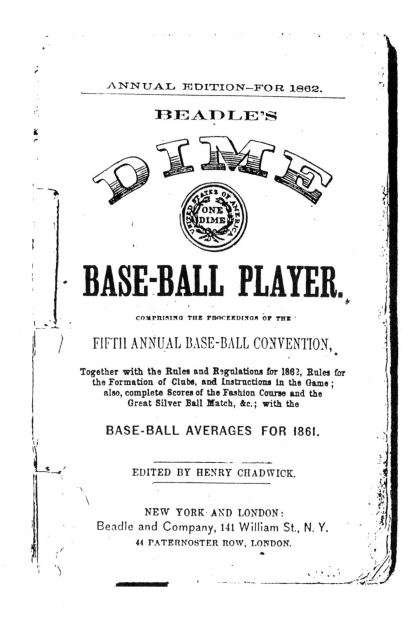

ANNUAL EDITION—FOR 1862.

BEADLE'S

DIME

ONE DIME

BASE-BALL PLAYER.

COMPRISING THE PROCEEDINGS OF THE

FIFTH ANNUAL BASE-BALL CONVENTION,

Together with the Rules and Regulations for 1862, Rules for the Formation of Clubs, and Instructions in the Game; also, complete Scores of the Fashion Course and the Great Silver Ball Match, &c.; with the

BASE-BALL AVERAGES FOR 1861.

EDITED BY HENRY CHADWICK.

NEW YORK AND LONDON:
Beadle and Company, 141 William St., N. Y.
44 PATERNOSTER ROW, LONDON.

other teams copied the style. The Knickerbockers wore dapper-looking blue pantaloons, white flannel shirts and straw hats (later on they changed to mohair caps and added wide patent-leather belts to their garb). Ironically, at no time did the Knickerbockers ever wear knickers! That style of baseball uniform didn't appear until 1869 when the Cincinnati Red Stockings burst onto the scene.

*This page from an unnamed 1859 publication heralds the nationwide spread of the exciting new game called Base Ball.*

24

THE CATCHER.

### THE NEW YORK GAME
#### OF
### BASE BALL.

THE game of Base Ball is fast becoming, in this country, what Cricket is to England, a national game, combining, as it does, exciting sport and healthful exercise at a trifling expense. It has a decided advantage over the monotonous routine of the Gymnasium or other modes of exercise.

The rules adopted by the National Association of Base Ball Players, who meet annually in New York, are rapidly being adopted by players in all parts of the country, they having been found superior to all others as giving a more equal share in the game to all the players engaged; as the game, when properly played, requires close attention, courage and activity; and the victory in a match depends as much upon the exellence of the fielding as on that of players in more prominent positions. The first Club formed in New England, under these rules, was organized June 16th, 1857, under the name of the "Tri-Mountain Base Ball Club of Boston," and for a long period was the only

3

# THE GAME GETS ORGANIZED

There came a need to form some kind of an organization to oversee the game and administrate the rules and regulations. In 1857 the Knickerbockers and over a dozen other clubs held a convention in New York City and a rules committee was set up. The following year another convention was held and 22 clubs attended. They formed themselves into the National Association of Base Ball Players, an organization which would govern the playing of baseball for the next thirteen years.

At the convention it was decided that, later that summer, a series of all-star games would be held between the best players from the New York teams and the best players from the Brooklyn teams. The first game, or "Great Base Ball Match" as it was billed, was held on July 20, 1858 at the Fashion Race Course, near Flushing, Long Island. Some 4000 spectators showed up to see New York defeat Brooklyn by a score of 22 to 18. An admission fee of 50 cents was charged to help recover the expenses of putting the grounds into shape for play. This is believed to be the first time admission was ever charged to a baseball game. (New York, by the way, went on to win the series two games to one.)

The first great baseball tour by a team from the New York City area took place during the summer of 1860 when the Excelsior club barnstormed throughout upper New York State, Pennsylvania, Maryland and Delaware. They finished the excursion undefeated, trouncing the local teams and stirring up interest in the game wherever they went.

356 FRANK LESLIE'S ILLUSTRATED NEWSPAPER. [AUGUST 2

BASE BALL MATCH FOR THE CHAMPIONSHIP BETWEEN THE ATLANTIC CLUB OF BROOKLYN AND THE MUTUAL CLUB OF NEW YORK, AT HOBOKEN, AUGUST 3—THE MUTUALS "CATCHING OUT" ATLANTICS ON A "FOUL BALL."

### BASE-BALL MATCH FOR THE CHAMPIONSHIP.

The Elysian Fields, at Hoboken, N. J., were crowded on the 3d inst., to witness the grand contest for the Championship of the United States, between the Mutual Club of New York and the Atlantic Club of Brooklyn. Never before was there such a vast assemblage of people gathered together on any similar occasion, and never has there been known in the annals of our national sports, such a closely contested game of base-ball, as that which took place on Thursday.

At a quarter to 4 P. M., all being in readiness for the match and the field clear—as well as it was possible to clear it—the contest commenced, the Atlantics being the first to go to the bat.

After some splendid play, which lasted one hour and a half, a heavy rainstorm put a stop to the sport. Five innings having been played according to the rules of the National Association, the game was decided in [ ] of the Atlantics. The score stood at the close—At[ ] 13; Mutuals, 12.

1865.

*Above: This illustrated newspaper account of a baseball game being played at Elysian Fields in 1865 depicts a championship match between the Brooklyn Atlantics and the New York Mutuals.*

*Left: The Ball Players' Chronicle was another early publication that helped to spread the word about baseball. This was just one of many early baseball publications that Henry Chadwick either edited or wrote for.*

*This is the 1865 edition of the Philadelphia Athletics, they were an amateur club at the time. The Athletic Base Ball Club has continuously existed in one form or another ever since 1860. In 1871 they would become founding members of the National Association of Professional Base Ball Players (the first professional league), then, in 1876, founding members of the National League. After being booted out of the N.L. at the end of it's first season they would later come back to play in the American Association, and after that in the American League, where they would eventually leave Philadelphia for Kansas City, and then move on to Oakland.*

# BASEBALL GOES TO WAR

The Civil War, from 1861 to 1865, played a major role in the spread of baseball nationally. Union soldiers from the northeast often played baseball for recreation behind the lines. Other Union soldiers and Confederate prisoners watched them and learned the game. And when the war was over, they took baseball home with them and taught it to others. The game spread like wildfire and soon people in cities and towns and on farms in all parts of the country were playing baseball. The game had definitely arrived!

During the latter half of the 1860s, teams sprouted up everywhere, from the small towns to the big cities, and it was along about this time that people began to see the commercial possibilities of the game. The concept of enclosing the field and then charging the spectators to enter the grounds, which had first begun on a regular basis at the Capitoline Grounds in Brooklyn in 1862, was becoming more and more prevalent.

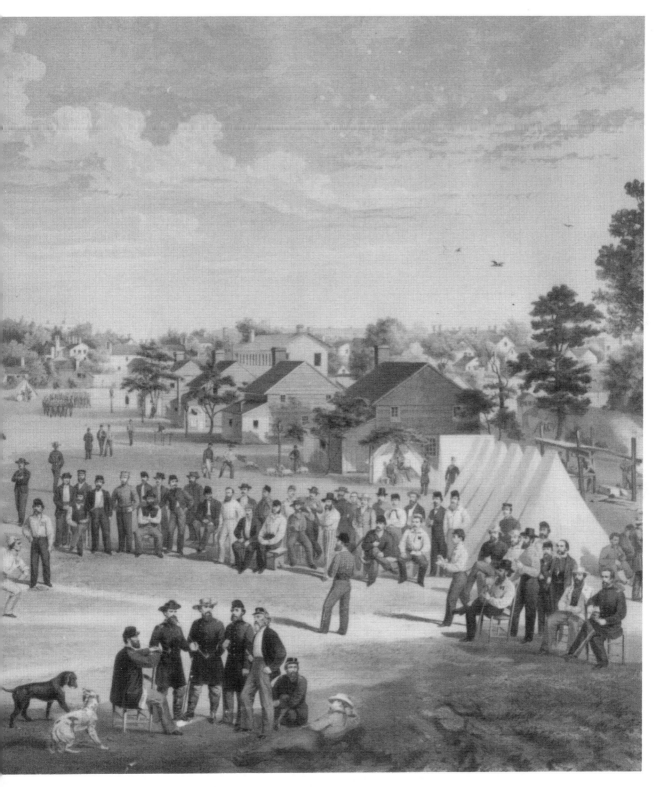

*This lithograph from the Civil War era shows Union prisoners playing baseball in a Confederate prison camp at Salisbury, North Carolina in 1862.*

*This Currier and Ives lithograph depicts the Grand Championship Match between the Philadelphia Athletics and the Brooklyn Atlantics, played on October 22, 1866 at the 15th and Columbia playing grounds in Philadelphia. Note the drunks and gamblers in the bottom of the picture. (Final score - Athletics 31, Atlantics 12).*

# THE GAME GETS ROWDIER

Baseball was no longer the gentleman's game that it was in Cartwright's day though. A rowdier element had taken over. Drinking and umpire baiting at games became commonplace. Open gambling, not only by the fans but by the players and even by the umpires, was prevalent. In many places women were strongly advised to stay away from the ballparks.

The players were generally considered to be amateurs, but many were paid for their services, either under the table or by having fake jobs arranged for them. To be considered a professional baseball player was bad form in those days. You were supposed to be playing for the fun of it — or at least pretending to. One example of this early hypocrisy took place in 1867 when 16-year-old pitching ace Al Spalding was offered a "job" as a clerk with a Chicago grocery wholesaler for $40 a week (which was about ten times the average wage for this type of work). This was not really a job at all, but an inducement to come to that city and pitch for Chicago's great Excelsior club. Meanwhile in New York City, the infamous "Boss" Tweed, who was president of the New York Mutuals from 1860 to 1871, put all his players on the city payroll, were they were usually listed as "street sweepers".

## THE FIRST TRUE PROFESSIONALS

All of this duplicity began to end in 1869, when a fellow by the name of Harry Wright who managed a baseball club in Cincinnati declared to the world that his team was indeed professional. The club, which wore bright red stockings made for them by a young lady named Margaret Truman, was called the Cincinnati Red Stockings. With a total annual payroll of $9300, they were the first openly-professional baseball team and that year they barnstormed all over the country, taking on all comers.

The English born Wright, a former professional cricket player and a jeweler by trade, had been hired by club

*Above: Team photograph of the 1869 Cincinnati Red Stockings. They were the first openly professional baseball team.*

*Opposite: The Red Stockings adorn the cover of a piece of sheet music. The composition was written in their honor.*

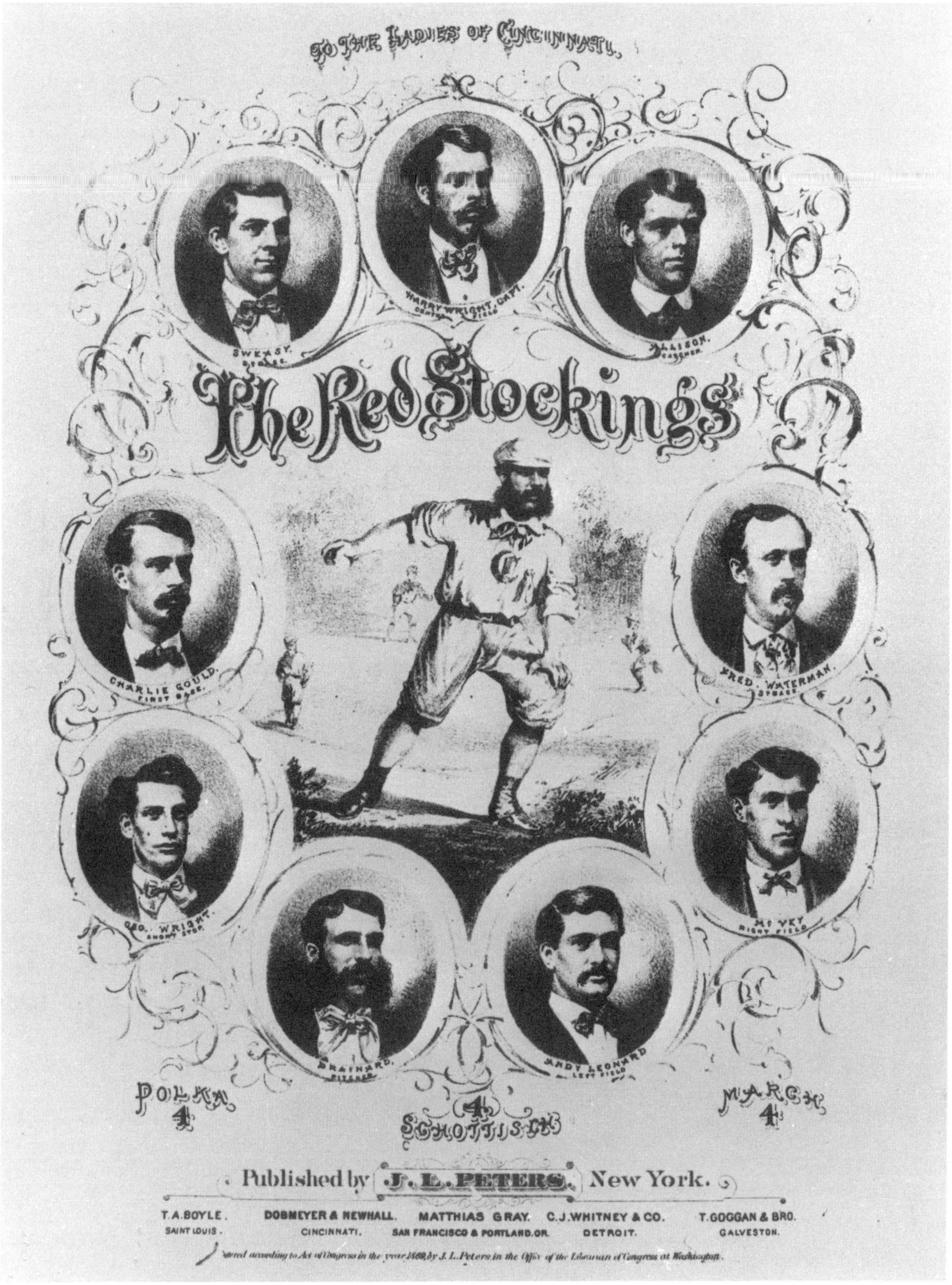
TO THE LADIES OF CINCINNATI.
SWEASY.
HARRY WRIGHT, CAPT.
ALLISON.
CATCHER.
The Red Stockings
CHARLIE GOULD.
FIRST BASE.
FRED. WATERMAN.
GEO. WRIGHT.
SHORT STOP.
McVEY
RIGHT FIELD
BRAINARD.
PITCHER
ANDY LEONARD
LEFT FIELD
POLKA
4
4
SCHOTTISCH
MARCH
4
Published by J. L. PETERS. New York.
T.A.BOYLE.
SAINT LOUIS.
DOBMEYER & NEWHALL.
CINCINNATI.
MATTHIAS GRAY.
SAN FRANCISCO & PORTLAND.OR.
C.J.WHITNEY & CO.
DETROIT.
T.GOGGAN & BRO.
GALVESTON.

president Aaron Champion to turn the Red Stockings into a top-caliber team. Harry Wright imported players from all over the country, including his brother George who was an all-star shortstop in New Jersey. The only player that was actually from Cincinnati was Charlie Gould, the first baseman.

The great Red Stockings national tour of 1869 took the team to such places as New York, Boston, Washington, Cleveland, Chicago, and as far west as San Francisco. They played the best local teams they could find and annihilated them all, ending up with a record of 56 wins and one tie. (The tie resulted when the Troy Haymakers walked off the field in the sixth inning with the scored tied 17-17 so that gamblers who had laid money on the Troy team could avoid paying off.)

The Red Stockings also revolutionized the way baseball players dressed — the spiffy knee-length flannel knickers and long stockings that they wore soon became the rage among ball clubs and replaced the traditional long trousers that dated back to the early days of the Knickerbocker Club.

The Cincinnati Red Stockings had become the acknowledged champions of the nation and by June of the follow-

*This drawing depicts the match between the Cincinnati Red Stockings and Brooklyn Atlantics, played in Brooklyn on June 14, 1870, in which the Atlantics ended the Red Stocking's 79 game unbeaten streak by edging them 8-7 in eleven innings.*

*This is a score sheet from the Cincinnati Red Stockings great nationwide tour of 1869. The Red Stockings completely annihilated all of the opposition and by June of the following year had put together a 79 game winning streak.*

ing year, 1870, they had stretched their winning streak to 79 when they were finally defeated by the Brooklyn Atlantics. Several other defeats later on in the season caused interest in the team to drop off at home, and this combined with the club's heavy travel expenses and mounting players salaries caused the demise of the team.

So Harry Wright packed up those bright red stockings the team had worn and moved to Boston where he formed the Boston Red Stockings. He took several Cincinnati players with him. And once again Harry Wright defied tradition and declared his new team to be professional. Almost at once the other great teams of the era cast off their amateur disguises, which brought about the era of the professional baseball league.

It was an era that would have a bumpy start though, for as we shall see in the next chapter, the first pro baseball league was destined to fail . . .

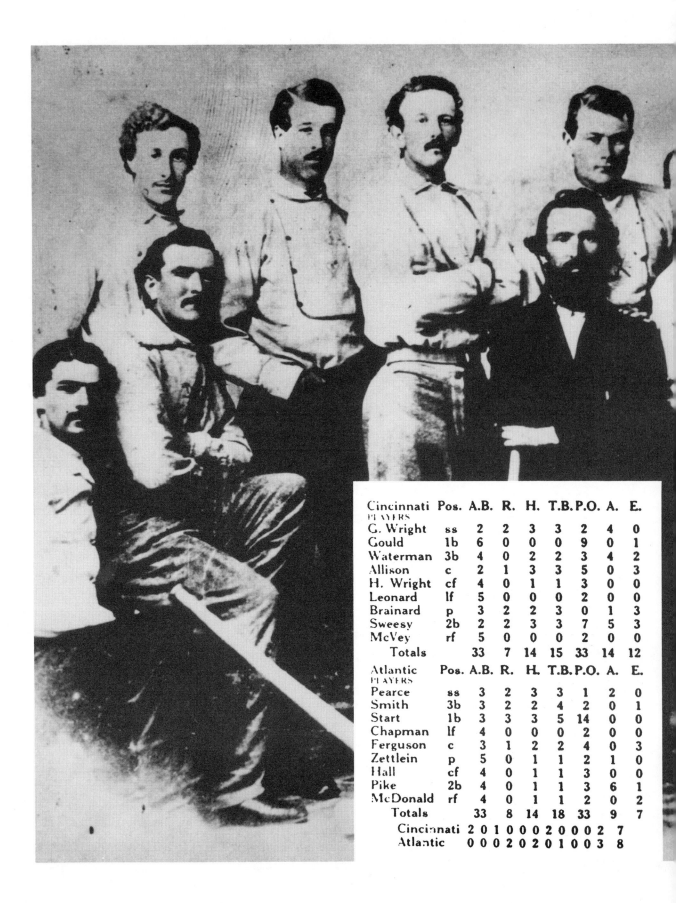

| Cincinnati PLAYERS | Pos. | A.B. | R. | H. | T.B. | P.O. | A. | E. |
|---|---|---|---|---|---|---|---|---|
| G. Wright | ss | 2 | 2 | 3 | 3 | 2 | 4 | 0 |
| Gould | 1b | 6 | 0 | 0 | 0 | 9 | 0 | 1 |
| Waterman | 3b | 4 | 0 | 2 | 2 | 3 | 4 | 2 |
| Allison | c | 2 | 1 | 3 | 3 | 5 | 0 | 3 |
| H. Wright | cf | 4 | 0 | 1 | 1 | 3 | 0 | 0 |
| Leonard | lf | 5 | 0 | 0 | 0 | 2 | 0 | 0 |
| Brainard | p | 3 | 2 | 2 | 3 | 0 | 1 | 3 |
| Sweesy | 2b | 2 | 2 | 3 | 3 | 7 | 5 | 3 |
| McVey | rf | 5 | 0 | 0 | 0 | 2 | 0 | 0 |
| Totals | | 33 | 7 | 14 | 15 | 33 | 14 | 12 |

| Atlantic PLAYERS | Pos. | A.B. | R. | H. | T.B. | P.O. | A. | E. |
|---|---|---|---|---|---|---|---|---|
| Pearce | ss | 3 | 2 | 3 | 3 | 1 | 2 | 0 |
| Smith | 3b | 3 | 2 | 2 | 4 | 2 | 0 | 1 |
| Start | 1b | 3 | 3 | 3 | 5 | 14 | 0 | 0 |
| Chapman | lf | 4 | 0 | 0 | 0 | 2 | 0 | 0 |
| Ferguson | c | 3 | 1 | 2 | 2 | 4 | 0 | 3 |
| Zettlein | p | 5 | 0 | 1 | 1 | 2 | 1 | 0 |
| Hall | cf | 4 | 0 | 1 | 1 | 3 | 0 | 0 |
| Pike | 2b | 4 | 0 | 1 | 1 | 3 | 6 | 1 |
| McDonald | rf | 4 | 0 | 1 | 1 | 2 | 0 | 2 |
| Totals | | 33 | 8 | 14 | 18 | 33 | 9 | 7 |

Cincinnati  2 0 1 0 0 0 2 0 0 0 2  7
Atlantic    0 0 0 2 0 2 0 1 0 0 3  8

### THE 1869 CINCINNATI RED STOCKINGS ROSTER AND PAYROLL

| | |
|---|---:|
| Harry Wright | |
| center field (and mgr) | $1200 |
| George Wright | |
| shortstop | 1400 |
| Asa Brainard | |
| pitcher | 1100 |
| Fred Waterman | |
| third base | 1000 |
| Charles Sweasy | |
| second base | 800 |
| Charles H. Gould | |
| first base | 800 |
| Douglas Allison | |
| catcher | 800 |
| Andrew J. Leonard | |
| left field | 800 |
| Calvin A. McVey | |
| right field | 800 |
| Richard Hurley | |
| substitute | 800 |
| **TOTAL** | **$9300** |

*This is a photograph of the Brooklyn Atlantics, the club that ended the Cincinnati Red Stockings' incredible winning streak. Inset at center is the score of that monumental game, which, as you will note, went into extra innings.*

# CHAPTER 4

# A NEW ERA BEGINS

On Saint Patrick's day, March 17, 1871, at Collier's Cafe on Broadway and Thirteenth Street in New York City, representatives from some of the best baseball clubs in the land gathered together to form the very first professional baseball league. They named their new creation the National Association of Professional Base Ball Players.

The league, which would begin play that summer, was composed of the Boston Red Stockings; the Chicago White Stockings; the New York Mutuals; the Philadelphia Ath-

*This 1873 drawing depicts baseball action in the early '70's. (It's reasonable to assume that this is a Philadelphia Athletics home game from the pennants that are flying above the grandstand, which would be in honor of Philadelphia's 1871 National Association championship).*

*A rare photo of two National Association of Professional Baseball Players teams. In 1872 the Philadelphia Athletics and the Boston Red Stockings pose for the camera just before the start of a game in Boston.*

letics; the Troy Haymakers; two clubs from Washington D.C., the Nationals and the Olympics; two clubs with the same nickname, the Cleveland Forest Citys and the Rockford Forest Citys; and the Fort Wayne Kekiongas. (The Kekiongas dropped out of the league in August and were replaced by the Brooklyn Ekfords.)

Unfortunately, the National Association turned out to be an embarrassment to all those who were associated with it. It was a loosely-knit organization renowned for its rowdiness, erratic schedule, open gambling on games, liquor-selling in parks, bribery and other forms of chicanery.

The league, which was in fact run by the players, lasted for only five years. The N.A. was characterized by such things as teams that would not honor their schedules late in the season when it meant travelling far from home, players that would jump from club to club (sometimes in midseason) and a lack of control of the games by umpires

*A team photo of the National Association's New York Mutuals taken sometime in the early 1870's.*

*Below: The New York Clipper was one of several publications that helped to publicize the game of baseball during the early years. The front page of the November 18, 1871 edition of this weekly newspaper features a story on the Philadelphia Athletics who just won the first National Association Championship (it was the only time in the N.A.'s five year existence that anyone else but Boston would take the pennant).*

## CHICAGO vs. BOSTON.

For the third time these clubs met on the grounds of the White Stockings on Monday, June 8, as noted in our past issue, and the result was the opposite of that in the two previous contests, as victory fell to the lot of the home nine, whose majority was five runs. The game was opened with the Reds at the bat, George Wright leading off with a safe hit, and being followed by Barnes, whose liner was held by Meyerle, and it being promptly sent to second, the first striker was put out, amid a tumult of applause. The next man flied out, and the Reds were ciphered. In their half of the first inning the Whites scored two runs, neither of which was earned, though three base-hits were made. The fielding of the Bostons was execrable. The second inning resulted in a blank on both sides, though errors were made by Devlin and Malone on the side of the Whites, and by Schafer on the other side. In the third inning the Bostons were blanked in quick order, Meyerle doing most of the fielding in fine style. The Whites scored two more on two base hits, and had errors by Schafer, Barnes and George Wright. The fourth inning was well fielded by the Chicagos, and the Bostons were blanked again, the Whites being retired in their half of the inning without getting a run. In the fifth inning the Reds managed to get two runs. They had made but two safe hits, but they received valuable assistance from Collins and Devlin, the former of whom pitched wildly. The Whites knocked out four, earning one of them on safe batting by Hines, Glenn, Cuthbert, Malone and Meyerle. Errors by Schafer and McVey and general bad throwing gave them the others. From this point the home club failed to score, the batting, as a rule, being weak, and the fielding of the opposing nine correspondingly accurate, but not remarkable. In the seventh inning the Bostons scored a run on two base-hits, and an accident to Glenn, in the right field, by which he tumbled into a pool of water. Neither scored afterwards, and the game closed at 8 to 3 in favor of the Whites, they having won it by outbatting, outfielding and outplaying their opponents at every point. The pitching of Collins, recently brought from St. Louis to act as a substitute, was rather wild, but nevertheless effective. Following is the score:

| BOSTON. | R. | 1B. | PO. | A. | E. | CHICAGO. | R. | 1B. | PO. | A. | E. |
|---|---|---|---|---|---|---|---|---|---|---|---|
| G. Wright, s s.. | 0 | 2 | 4 | 5 | 1 | Cuthbert, l f.... | 2 | 3 | 2 | 0 | 0 |
| Barnes, 2d b.... | 0 | 0 | 1 | 5 | 1 | Force, s s...... | 0 | 1 | 2 | 4 | 0 |
| White, r f....... | 0 | 2 | 0 | 0 | 0 | Malone, c...... | 2 | 1 | 4 | 0 | 3 |
| Spalding, p .... | 0 | 0 | 0 | 5 | 0 | Meyerle, 3d b.. | 1 | 4 | 1 | 3 | 1 |
| McVey, c...... | 0 | 1 | 3 | 2 | 2 | Devlin, 1st b... | 1 | 1 | 17 | 1 | 2 |
| Leonard, l f.... | 0 | 2 | 5 | 0 | 2 | Peters, 2d b.... | 0 | 1 | 1 | 3 | 0 |
| O'Rourke, 1st b. | 0 | 0 | 12 | 0 | 0 | Hines, c. f..... | 1 | 1 | 0 | 0 | 0 |
| H. Wright, c f.. | 1 | 1 | 1 | 2 | 0 | Glenn, r f...... | 0 | 2 | 0 | 0 | 0 |
| Schafer, 3d b... | 2 | 1 | 1 | 3 | 8 | Collins, p...... | 1 | 0 | 0 | 3 | 4 |
| Totals ...... | 3 | 9 | 27 | 18 | 14 | Totals ...... | 8 | 14 | 27 | 14 | 10 |

Boston.......... 0 0 0 0 0 2 0 1 0—3
Chicago......... 2 0 2 0 4 0 0 0 0—8

Runs earned—Reds, 0; Whites, 1. First base on errors—Reds, 3; Whites, 9. Left on bases—Reds, 7; Whites, 14. Passed balls—Malone, 3; McVey, 1. Wild pitches—Collins, 6 Umpire—Thomas Foley. Time—2h. 25m.

*This clipping from the June 20, 1874 edition of the New York Clipper gives an account of a rather error filled (24 in total) National Association game between the Boston Red Stockings and the Chicago White Stockings played on June 8 in Chicago. The White Stockings won the game by the score of 8 to 3 by apparently "outbatting, outfielding and outplaying their opponents at every point". I guess we'll never know how big the pool of water that Chicago right fielder Glenn fell into was, or exactly where it was located.*
*Above Right: The National Association standings as of June 15, 1874.*

## CHAMPIONSHIP RECORD.

The championship record up to June 15, inclusive, is as follows:

| | Games Played. | Won. | Lost. |
|---|---|---|---|
| Boston......................... | 25 | 20 | 5 |
| Athletic........................ | 20 | 12 | 8 |
| Mutual......................... | 20 | 11 | 9 |
| Chicago........................ | 12 | 6 | 6 |
| Philadelphia.................... | 15 | 7 | 8 |
| Hartford....................... | 14 | 6 | 8 |
| Baltimore...................... | 22 | 5 | 17 |
| Atlantic........................ | 14 | 4 | 10 |
| Totals ....................142 | | 71 | 69 |

The clubs are given in the order of won games, as it is by the number of victories won that the pennant is awarded, and not by the percentage of won games:

| | Athletic. | Atlantic. | Baltimore. | Boston. | Chicago. | Hartford. | Mutual. | Philadelphia. | Games won. |
|---|---|---|---|---|---|---|---|---|---|
| Athletic........... | .. | 2 | 2 | 0 | 1 | 1 | 2 | 4 | 12 |
| Atlantic........... | 0 | | 2 | 2 | 0 | 0 | 0 | 0 | 4 |
| Baltimore......... | 2 | 1 | | 2 | 0 | 1 | 0 | 0 | 5 |
| Boston............ | 2 | 3 | 3 | | 2 | 2 | 4 | 4 | 20 |
| Chicago.......... | 1 | 0 | 2 | 1 | | 2 | 0 | 0 | 6 |
| Hartford.......... | 1 | 2 | | 0 | 0 | | 1 | 0 | 6 |
| Mutual............ | 3 | 1 | 4 | 1 | 2 | 1 | | 0 | 11 |
| Philadelphia..... | 0 | 1 | 2 | 0 | 1 | 1 | 2 | .. | 7 |
| Games lost....... | 8 | 10 | 17 | 5 | 6 | 8 | 9 | 8 | 71 |

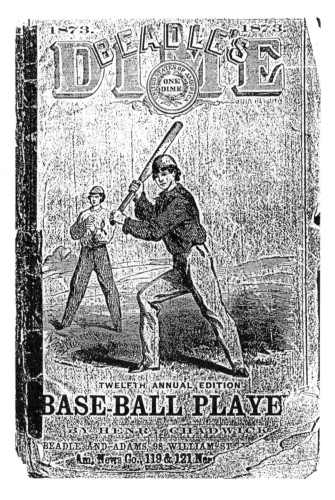

*The cover of the 1873 edition of Beadle's Base-Ball Player, another one of the early publications that helped to popularize baseball.*

who were usually unpaid. There was a turnover of some 25 or so clubs in the five years that the league existed, and one team (Harry Wright's Boston Red Stockings) was so powerful that it totally dominated all opposition, winning the league championship four out of five years.

The demise of the National Association was brought about by Chicago club president William Hulbert, who lead a movement to replace the floundering Association with a new league, a league that would turn the organized game back into a pastime that decent folk would not be ashamed to bring their families to watch. His would be a tightly organized league where the play would be honest

*The Boston Red Stockings won the National Association championship four out of the five years that the league was in existence. Sitting in the center of this 1875 team photo is manager Harry Wright. Standing second from right in photo and holding a ball in his hand, is young pitching ace Al Spalding. He would later go on to become a baseball executive, manufacturer of sporting equipment, and promoter of the Doubleday myth.*

*After managing the Cincinnati Red Stockings, the first truly professional baseball team, Harry Wright moved on to Boston. Here he poses in his Boston Red Stockings uniform.*

. . . a league that would keep to a firm schedule of games . . . a league that would be an organization — not of baseball players, but of baseball clubs, with the final authority in the hands of management.

# THE N.L. TAKES OVER

On February 2, 1876, at the Grand Central Hotel in New York City, William Hulbert and delegates from other clubs gathered together to form a new league. And the National Association was replaced by the National League of Professional Base Ball Clubs.

The National League immediately banned open gambling and liquor sales at games, vowed to expel clubs that failed to stick to schedules and later on even prohibited the playing of league games on Sunday.

It was agreed that written contracts between clubs and players were to be respected, thereby ending the practice of teams pirating players away from each other. Only cities with populations of at least 75,000 would be eligible for franchises in this new venture. Umpires were to be paid. An admission fee of 50 cents to all league games was set.

The National League started out with eight clubs: the Philadelphia Athletics, Boston Red Caps, Hartford Dark Blues and New York Mutuals in the east; and the Cincinnati Red Stockings, Louisville Grays, St. Louis Brown Stockings and Chicago White Stockings in the west.

There is also a more cynical view of Hulbert's motives for founding the new league. In 1875 Hulbert made a deal with Boston superstar pitcher Al Spalding to have Spalding jump to the Chicago club the following year, not only to pitch, but to act as captain and manager of the team as well. Hulbert then got Spalding to persuade fellow Boston teammates Cal McVey, Ross Barnes and Deacon Brown, who were the very heart of the Red Stockings lineup, to join him in his defection to the White Stockings. And if this wasn't enough, Hulbert and Spalding also made a deal with Adrian "Cap" Anson, the Philadelphia Athletic's young slugger to jump ship to the Chicago club when the next season began.

It was the very first wholesale defection of baseball stars, and a number of baseball historians contend that

*Opposite: William Hulbert, the Chicago White Stockings president who was instrumental in the founding of the the National League.*

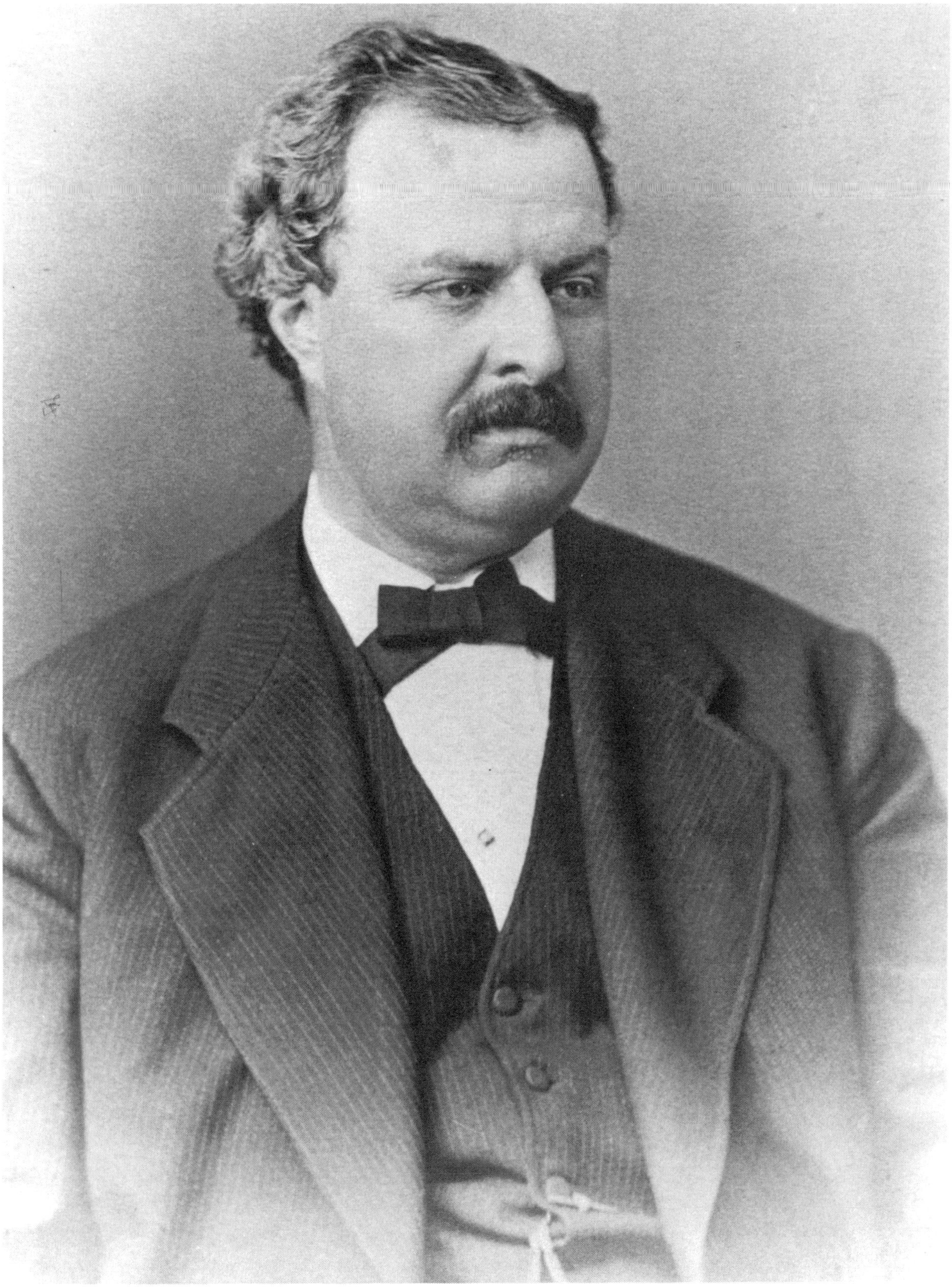

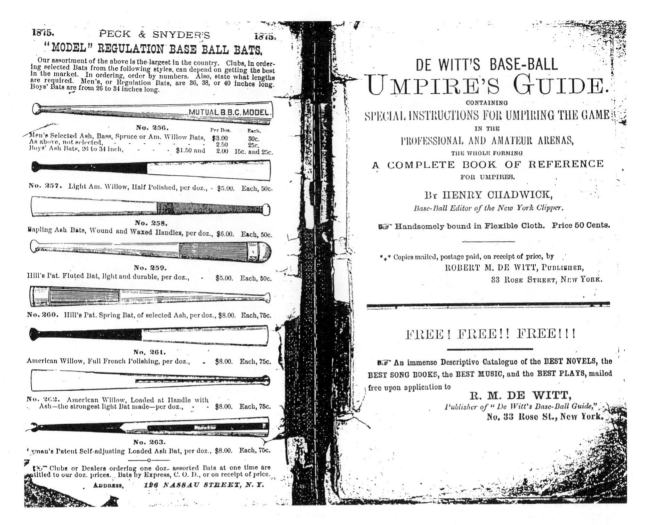

Hulbert feared the National Association would expel the White Stockings for his act of gross piracy, so he avoided a confrontation by forming a new league.

No matter what Hulbert's true intentions were, in one fell swoop, he did, in fact, clean up baseball and create a respectable new league that has remained in business for well over a hundred years.

The first National League game was played in Philadelphia on April 22, 1876 before 3000 fans, with the Boston Red Caps defeating the Philadelphia Athletics by the score of 6 to 5. At the end of the season Hulbert's Chicago White Stockings took the first N.L. pennant with a record of 52 wins and 14 losses.

*In the 1875 edition of Dewitt's Base-Ball Guide, among other things, you could find out how to order baseball bats for 50 cents each (or five dollars for a dozen) or how to obtain a special Umpire's Guide for a mere 50 cents.*

*Opposite: The National League was born on February 2, 1876. Here is how two of America's top newspapers of the day, the Chicago Tribune and the New York Daily Graphic, heralded the event.*

# THE DIAMOND SQUARED.

## And an Honest Base-Ball Associ-ation Born into the World,

## Which Required that the Philadelphia and Like Clubs Be Disfel-lowshiped.

## Grand Council of Delegates from the Representative Clubs at New York.

## Adoption of Constitution and Rules for the Centennial Year.

## Progress of the Female Pedestrians at the Sec-ond Regiment Armory.

### BASE-BALL.
#### A NEW ERA.
##### *Special Dispatch to The Chicago Tribune.*

NEW YORK, Feb. 3.—The most important measure ever adopted by the professional base-ball clubs of this country has been considered and approved by a council of representatives of the eight principal clubs of the country, in ses-sion at the Grand Central Hotel.

The new scheme, which is destined to elevate base-ball to the rank of a legitimate amusement, is the formation of a new association of profes-sional clubs on the debris of the old National As-sociation, and the clubs which participate are the Bostons, of Boston ; the Hartfords, of Hart-ford ; the Mutuals, of New York ; the Athletics, of Philadelphia ; the White Stockings, of Chica-go ; the Cincinnatis, of Cincinnati ; the Louis-villes, of Louisville ; and the St. Louis, of St. Louis.

The last-named four clubs were represented at this conference by W. A. Hulbert, President of the Chicagos, and Mr. Fowle, of the St. Louis Club. The Eastern clubs were all represented by delegates.

#### THE CONFERENCE

met yesterday noon at the Grand Central Hotel, and organized by the election of Nick Young as Secretary, after which the Western delegates stated the proposition for a new association more fully than it had been given by letter, and pro-ceeded to enumerate the advantages to be gained by the proposed union.

As nearly as I could get at the reasons, they were these :

*First*—The feeling that something must be done to get rid of the dishonest players who have brought disrepute on the game. It was pointed out that the present Association had been proved powerless to properly govern the game, be-cause it had been run by unscrupulous men, who had been willing to resort to any meannesses to compass their ends. As a sample of this the conduct of the Atlantics

---

# THE DAILY GRAPHIC
· FRIDAY, FEBRUARY 4, 1876.

## NO MORE BASE-BALL GAMBLING.

#### EIGHT OF THE MOST PROMINENT CLUBS WITHDRAWN FROM THE NATIONAL ASSOCI-ATION—A LEAGUE IN THE INTEREST OF HONESTY AND FAIR PLAY ORGANIZED.

The decline of professional base ball in public favor has hardly been less rapid than its rise. The very general conviction that players sold themselves out and "threw" their games has served to kill the interest once felt in the result of matches between the leading clubs. But a few years ago the games at the Union or Capitoline grounds were as popular as the races at Jerome or Prospect Park; where the specta-tors numbered thousands then they barely reach into the hundreds now. Jockeying for gate money and playing into the hands of the pool-sellers has had its legitimate effect.

Recently steps have been taken towards effecting a reform that should revive the public interest in the game by restoring the public confidence, and at a meeting of the representatives of leading clubs in the East and West at the Grand Central Hotel on Wednes-day a new combination or organization was formed, to be known as the National League of Pro-fessional Base-ball Clubs. This is to be entirely dis-tinct from the old organization—the National As-sociation of Professional Base ball Players—and in-cludes the Athletics, Bostons, Hartfords, and Mutuals from the East, and the Chicago, Cincinnati, Louis-ville, and St. Louis clubs from the West. It will be no-ticed that but a single club is allowed in the new or-ganization from the same city or locality. Mr. M. G. Bulkley, of the Hartford Club, was elected Presi-dent and Mr. N. E. Young, of Washington, Secre-tary.

The league discussed in detail the abuses that have crept into the management of professional clubs and games, and revised in the most thorough manner the code of playing rules that govern the National Asso-ciation. The new regulations are as stringent as the combined experience and judgment of the veterans present could frame, and have been constructed to cover any and every violation of faith or honor that can arise. The league will be governed by a board of five directors. Those chosen for the current year are from the Boston, Hartford, Louisville, Mutual, and St. Louis clubs. These five directors will sit annually as a board of appeals to decide all disputed points, and their decision is to be final.

One of the most flagrant abuses of the old associa-tion was the ease with which a player expelled from one club for misdemeanor could reinstate himself despite the knowledge of his misconduct. If he had any exceptional ability as a player his services were invariably demanded by a rival club of that from which he had been driven, and an appeal to the National Board, provided the club was influen-tial enough, would give him the right to play. Under the code of the new organization, if there is reason to suspect that a player is guilty of corrupt practices, charges may be preferred against him by any one included in the league to the Secretary of the league. The secretary will notify the club to which the suspected member belongs, and the club must investigate and take action upon the charges within a specified time. In case this is delayed or nothing is done in the matter the club is held responsible, and will go out of the organization under the rules. In all trials of players the Board of Directors sit as final judges, and from their decision there is no appeal. A

# The Finest Game of Base Ball Ever Witnessed in Louisville.

## It Was Played Yesterday, the Mighty Chicagoes and the Home Nine Being Contestants.

## But Though Our Side Lost by 4 to 0, Yet There Was No Disgrace In't.

## Six Thousand People Make the Welkin Ring With Their Applause.

## How the Game Was Lost and How it Was Won—Not a Run Earned.

## Presentation of Medals to the Louisville Club in the Presence of the Admiring Throng.

### A COMPLETE REPORT.

The base-ball season opened in Louisville yesterday amid auspices of the most flattering nature. The skies were smiling in their loveliest azure, while the atmosphere was agreeably tempered with the softest zephyrs of the spring-tide. The 25th of April has for many months been anticipated in Louisville with the liveliest interest. Since this date was fixed for the inauguration of the summer's sport it had with its gradual approach become more and more to be regarded in the nature of a holiday event. Considering the multitude of admirers which the game may claim among the people of the Falls Cities, and the local pride which is everywhere felt in the players composing the Louisville professional nine, the occasion would not have been adequately commemorated had the home club entered the lists with less noble antagonists than the Chicago nine of 1876. This organization is the most expensive in the land. The individual players command, in some instances, salaries which seem almost fabulous. The array of names presents a glittering constellation. White, Spalding, Barnes, McVey—what giants they are!

## SPORTING NEWS.

### The White Stockings Beaten by the Hartfords Yesterday, 4 to 1.

*Special Dispatch to The Tribune.*

HARTFORD, Conn., May 25.—The White Stockings played their fourteenth championship game of the year here to-day, and scored their third defeat, the Hartfords out-batting them from the start to the finish. About 1,200 people were present. The scoring began in the second inning, when Ferguson led off with a clean hit, and was sent to third by York's two-baser, after Carey and Bond had been retired. Mills helped matters very much by a clean hit to left, which let Ferguson home. Glenn returned the ball to Anson, and he sent it home to catch York, but White failed to hold it, and two runs were scored. The Whites could only offset this with one tally made in the third inning by Glenn, who led off with a clean hit, stole second and third, and got over the plate on Hines' long fly to Remsen. The home club took another run in the sixth inning, Higham getting first on Anson's error, and around home on

SEVERAL JUGGLES AND A PASSED BALL,

aided by a safe hit by Carey. In the seventh inning, Mills hit safely, and was sent to third by Harbidge's hit, which Hines did not handle cleanly. When Harbidge started for second, White sent a hot shot to Barnes to cut him off, but overthrew, and of course Mills scored. A series of bad errors of judgment in the seventh inning prevented the Whites from getting several runs. Anson led off with a base on called balls, and McVey sent him to second on a safe hit. Spalding followed with a hit to Burdock, which the latter fumbled, but finally got to second in time to catch McVey, though the decision was unquestionably

AN ERROR OF THE UMPIRE.

Carey kept the ball in his hand, and completely fooled Anson, who played off from third, and was caught in a foolish manner. Addy then took first, and Spalding third on an error by Ferguson, but White ended matters by a liner to Carey. The score does not show the character of the batting, which was hard and strong by the Whites, but also unpleasantly unlucky. Hines, for instance, hit three long line drives just where some one was waiting for him, and Anson, McVey, and White were similarly unlucky in having what seemed safe line hits fly right at a fielder. The Hartfords played about the same game as on Tuesday, full of foolish plays and open recrimination between the players. Following is

THE SCORE:

| Chicago. | T | R | B | P | A | E |
|---|---|---|---|---|---|---|
| Barnes, 2 b.... | 5 | 0 | 2 | 3 | 4 | 1 |
| Hines, c. f..... | 4 | 0 | 0 | 3 | 0 | 1 |
| Anson, 3 b..... | 4 | 0 | 0 | 2 | 2 | 2 |
| McVey, 1 b.... | 4 | 0 | 2 | 9 | 0 | 0 |
| Spalding, p.... | 3 | 0 | 0 | 2 | 0 | 0 |
| Addy, r. f..... | 3 | 0 | 0 | 1 | 0 | 0 |
| White, c...... | 3 | 0 | 0 | 7 | 0 | 3 |
| Peters, s. s.... | 4 | 0 | 0 | 1 | 1 | 0 |
| Glenn, l. f..... | 4 | 1 | 1 | 2 | 0 | 0 |
| Total...... | 35 | 1 | 5 | 27 | 8 | 7 |
| Hartford. | | | | | | |
| Burdock, 2 b.... | 5 | 0 | 0 | 2 | 0 | 0 |
| Remsen, c. f.... | 4 | 0 | 0 | 3 | 1 | 0 |
| Higham, r. f.... | 4 | 1 | 0 | 0 | 0 | 0 |
| Ferguson, 3 b.... | 4 | 1 | 1 | 3 | 2 | 3 |
| Carey, s. s.... | 4 | 0 | 1 | 3 | 5 | 1 |
| Bond, p..... | 4 | 0 | 2 | 0 | 1 | 2 |
| York, l. f..... | 4 | 1 | 1 | 5 | 0 | 0 |
| Mills, 1 b.... | 4 | 1 | 3 | 5 | 0 | 1 |
| Harbidge, c.... | 4 | 0 | 1 | 6 | 0 | 0 |
| Totals...... | 37 | 4 | 9 | 27 | 7 | 7 |

| Innings— | 1 | 2 | 3 | 4 | 5 | 6 | 7 | 8 | 9 | |
|---|---|---|---|---|---|---|---|---|---|---|
| Chicago | 0 | 0 | 1 | 0 | 0 | 0 | 0 | 0 | 0— | 1 |

*Far Left: The Louisville Greys hosted the Chicago White Stockings on April 25, 1876 in the first National League game ever played in Louisville. Here is an excerpt from an account of the game that was published in a local newspaper.*
*Note - The Louisville Greys folded at the end of the following season. They were replaced in the N.L. in '78 by the Providence Greys.*

*Close Left: When the Hartford Dark Blues hosted the Chicago White Stockings for an National League contest played on May 25, 1876, here's how the Chicago Tribune reported the game in their May 26 edition. There was a total of 14 errors in the game (7 for each side) and there was only one earned run, of the five that were scored (it was credited to Hartford). It seems that Chicago's batting was "hard and strong" but alas, it was also "unpleasantly unlucky" and as a result, even though Hartford played a game "full of foolish plays and open recrimination between the players", the White Stockings lost by a score of 4 - 1.*

*Right: In the early years Dewitt's Base-Ball Guides contained the rules of baseball as well as tips on how to play the game... this is the cover of the 1877 edition.*

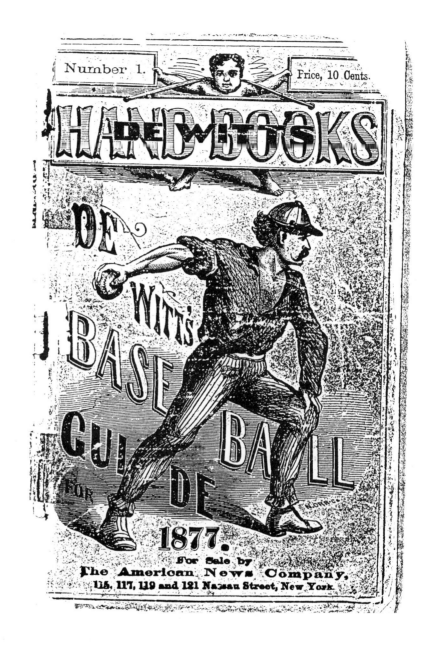

In the winter following that first season of '76, William Hulbert took over the presidency of the league. He was determined to run a tight ship and the first thing he did was to throw both the New York and Philadelphia clubs out of the league for failing to make their final western road trips at the end of the season. (Neither city was admitted back into the league until 1883.) In 1877 it was discovered that four Louisville players had conspired to throw the pennant to Boston. Hulbert banned the players from baseball for life. In 1880 he booted Cincinnati out of the league for selling beer at home games and leasing their park to teams that played on Sunday.

In the first few years of the N.L., the road was rather rocky. Almost all the clubs lost money, and Hartford, St. Louis and Louisville dropped out before the start of the '78 season, to be replaced by Providence, Indianapolis and Milwaukee. The latter two clubs dropped out in '79 and four new teams — Cleveland, Buffalo, Troy and Syracuse — then joined. Franchises would come and go (in its first 25 years of existence some 21 cities were represented in the National League at one time or another), yet the league survived due to stern, uncompromising management and the solid foundation that was laid down by Hulbert and the rest of the men who established the league.

# TAKE ME OUT TO AN OLD TIME BALLPARK

What were the ballparks like during the latter part of the '70s? Well, they were quite small (usually holding anywhere from 1,500 to 4,000 spectators) and generally not constructed in a very durable fashion, as the owners had no reason to believe that the National League would stay in business for very long. According to Bill James in his *Historical Baseball Abstract*, the owners usually "bought some wood and threw up fences and primitive bleachers and maybe a clubhouse or a dugout; the players often assisted in the construction. In a couple of years the thing fell down or burned down or rotted out, or they just got tired of it and built another one." Clubs would sometimes switch home ballparks in mid season.

# BASEBALL ~1878

*A baseball game underway at the New York Polo Grounds in 1878.*

8     SPALDING'S

seems to have the ball in the hollow of his hand, no matter how he expects to curve it. Most players, however, hold the ball differently for each delivery.

The first illustration gives the delivery used for the in-curve by Reis, of the Chicago Club. He closes the

Position of Hand for the In-Curve to a Right-Hand Batter, or Out-Curve to a Left-Hand Batter.

third and last fingers, and holds the ball with the first and second and the thumb. Raising his hand nearly to the height of the shoulder and back of him, he takes a step forward, and, bringing his hand down even with his waist,

BASE-BALL GUIDE.     9

delivers the ball with his wrist turned well back and a sort of snap motion which can be compared to nothing so well as to the "cracking" of a whip. The whole point in this delivery is to have the ball leave the two fingers last. It should, in fact, roll off those fingers, as one might say, and thus get a rotary motion, which will give it the curve. This will be made clear enough by taking a ball in the hand and allowing it to roll off the fingers to the side.

The second illustration presents the method of delivery used in the out-curve. It appears more difficult than the

Position of Hand for the Out-Curve to Right-Hand Batters, or In-Curve to Left-Hand Batters.

# THE BEER BALL LEAGUE

The N.L. was beginning to gain steady ground in the early 1880s, when it suddenly faced competition. In 1882, a rival league called the American Association was formed.

This new league began with six clubs which were located in Cincinnati, Philadelphia, Pittsburgh, St. Louis, Louisville and Baltimore. The following year they would add New York and Columbus.

The American Association, which lasted for nine years and was also called "the beer ball league," started out by cutting ticket prices from 50 to 25 cents, scheduling games on Sundays and allowing beer to be sold in the stands.

*This 1878 edition of Spalding's Official Base-Ball Guide gives instructions on how to throw a curve ball underhanded (pitchers weren't allowed to throw overhand until 1883).*

Ron McCulloch / 65

After an initial skirmish, the National League decided to try and co-exist with the new league and they worked out a document called the National Agreement which led to mutual protection over players' contracts and brought about the first post-season series between league champions in 1884. In this premiere edition of the World Series, the N.L.'s Providence Greys, led by the pitching of Charles "Old Hoss" Radbourn, defeated the A.A. champion New York Metropolitans in three straight games, in a best out of five series.

*In 1879 you could outfit a baseball player with a whole uniform, including shoes for between $7.00 and $9.00, according to this ad that appeared in the 1879 edition of Dewitt's Base-Ball Guide.*

*Above: The National League's New York Gothams pose for a team photo in 1884. In 1885 they would become known as the Giants.*

*Right: The 1880 edition of Dewitt's Base-Ball Guide gave illustrated instructions on how to play the game.*

# HIGHLIGHTS OF THE 1880s

The 1880s was the decade when professional baseball truly captured the hearts and minds of the nation. Daily newspapers all across the land were now printing accounts of big time baseball on a regular basis, and assigning reporters to cover the game full-time.

In the '80s the game itself went through several major changes: in 1881 the pitching distance was increased from 45 to 50 feet, and then two years later, in 1883, pitchers were allowed to throw overhand, giving them a tremendous advantage over the batters, as the pitching distance was still ten and a half feet closer to the plate than it is now. During this era, the average pitcher would win between 20 and 50 games a season depending on the quality of the team behind him.

"Old Hoss" Radburn, using a cricket-style pitching motion that included a running start, won 60 out of the 73

THE BASE-BALL GUIDE.

THE CORRECT POSITION IN BATTING.

THE BASE-BALL GUIDE.

A BAD POSITION IN BATTING.

CINCINNATIS.
CHAMPIONS 1882.
(AMERICAN ASSOCIATION.)

games he pitched in for Providence in their world championship year of 1884. Also in '84, Guy Jackson Heckler, pitching for the American Association's Louisville Eclipse, finished the season with a record of 52 wins and 20 losses, and over in the National League, the Buffalo Bison's James F. Galvin had a 1884 record of 46 wins and 21 losses (this followed a 44 - 29 record the previous year).

Gloves specifically designed for fielding purposes were introduced in the mid-1880s (gloves intended for the protection of the hands only, had been worn as early as 1878). Masks and chest protectors for catchers were also adopted during this era.

*The Cincinnati team that won the American Association championship in 1882.*

Metropolitans 1882

New York

*Above: They were the original New York Mets! The American Association's New York Metropolitans pose for a team photo in 1882.*

*Right: St. George's Cricket Field on Staten Island where the New York Metropolitans played their home games in the mid 1880's.*

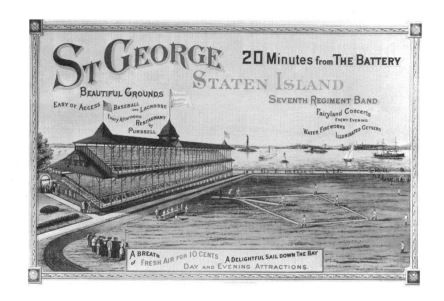

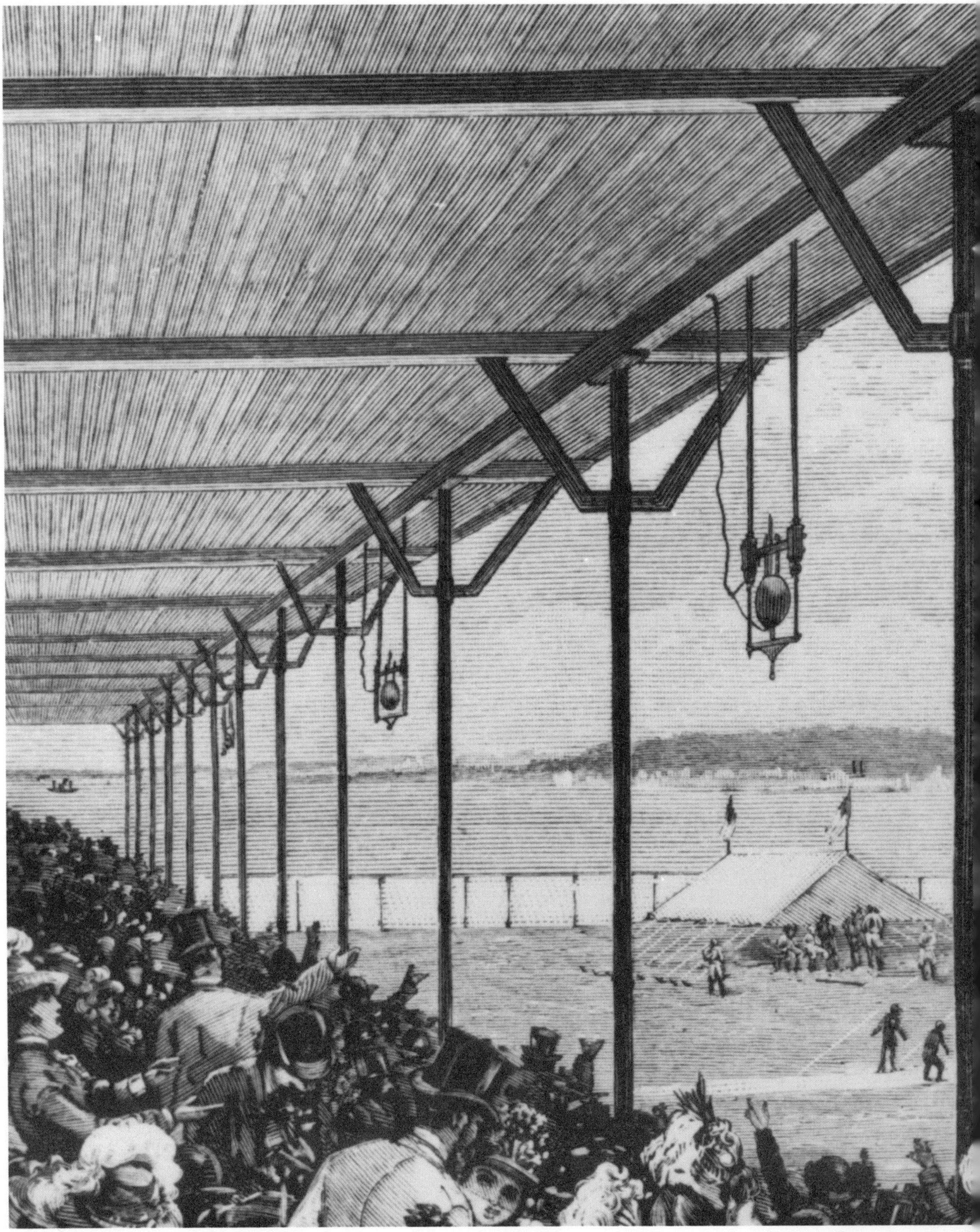

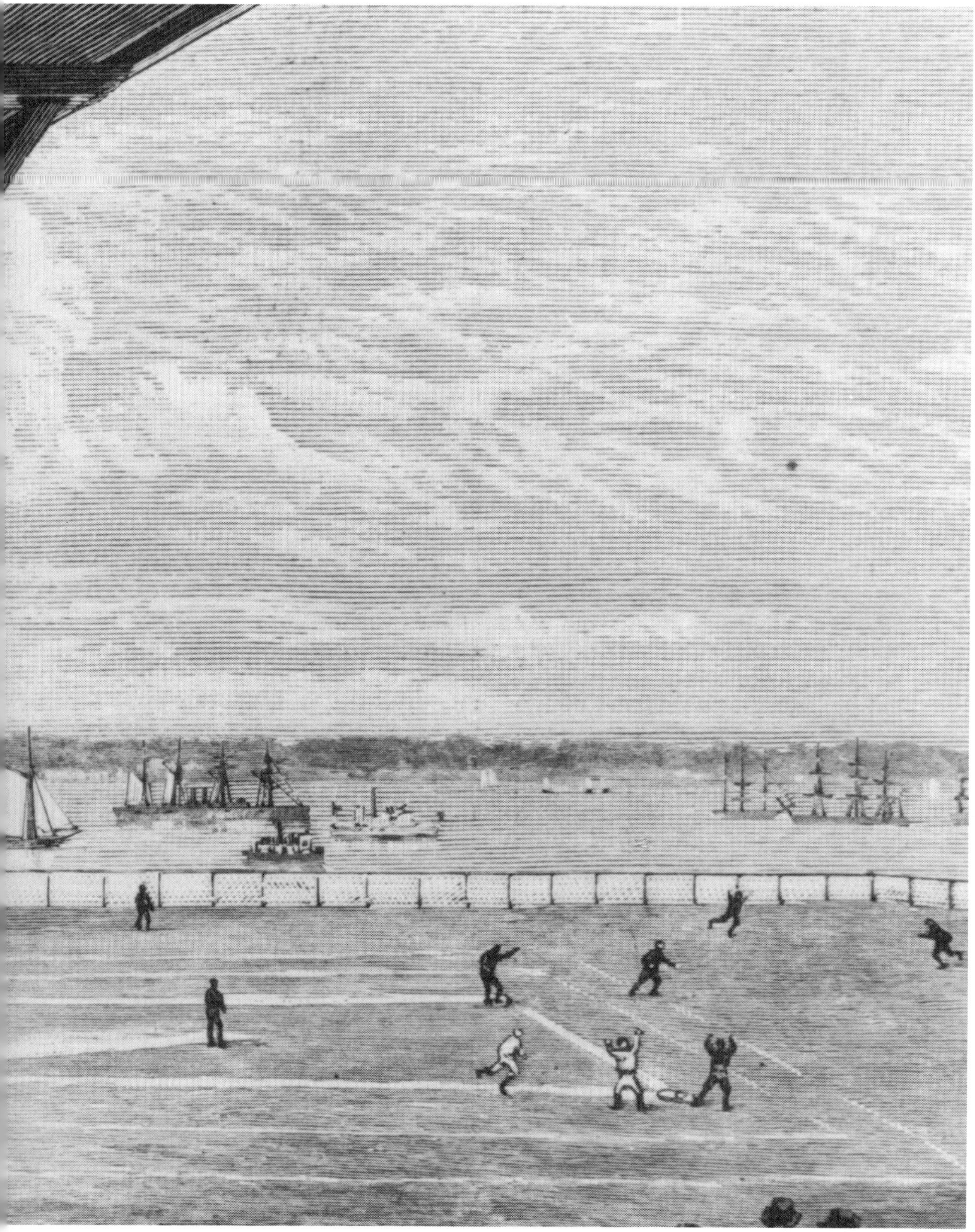

Up until 1887, a batter had the right to request the pitcher to throw either a high or a low pitch. It took nine balls to get a batter to first at the start of the decade, seven in 1882, five in 1887, and finally four in 1889. In 1888 the three-strike rule was finally adopted. (During the previous season, it took four strikes to get a batter out.)

It was the era when the bunt first became a major part of offensive strategy. Bats with one side flattened were

**SPALDING'S TRADE-MARKED CATCHER'S MASKS.—Continued.**

No. 1-0. SPALDING'S REGULATION LEAGUE MASK, made of heavy wire, well-padded and faced with horsehide, warranted first-class in every respect.................................$3 00

No. 1. SPALDING'S BOYS' LEAGUE MASK, made of heavy wire, equally as heavy in proportion to size as the No. 2-0 mask. It is made to fit a boy's face and gives the same protection as the League Mask...................................................2 50

## AMATEUR MASKS.

To meet the demand for good masks at a low price, we have manufactured a line of amateur masks, which are superior to any mask in the market at the same price. We do not guarantee these masks, and believe that our Trade-Marked Masks are worth more than the difference in price.

No. A. AMATEUR MASK, made the same size and general style as the League Mask, but with lighter wire and faced with leather (we guarantee this mask to be superior to so-called League or professional masks sold by other manufacturers).....................$1 75

No. B. BOYS' AMATEUR MASK, similar to No. A Mask, only made smaller to fit a boy's face.......................1 50

Amateur Mask.

Any of the above masks mailed post-paid on receipt of price.

## SPALDING'S TRADE-MARKED CATCHER'S GLOVES.

After considerable expense and many experiments we have finally perfected a Catcher's Glove that meets with general favor from professional catchers.

The old style of open backed gloves introduced by us several years ago is still adhered to, but the quality of material and workmanship has been materially improved, until now we are justified in claiming the best line of catcher's gloves in the market. These gloves do not interfere with throwing, can be easily put on and taken off, and no player subject to sore hands should be without a pair. Our new patent seamless palm glove is admittedly the finest glove ever made, and is used by all professional catchers. We make them in ten different grades, as follows:

No. 4-0. SPALDING'S SPECIAL LEAGUE CATCHER'S GLOVE. Patented, full left hand. Made from choice soft buck-kin, padded and lined with kid. Soft leather tips on fingers of left glove. This is the finest fielder's glove ever produced. Each pair packed in separate box.

Per pair..........$5 00

No. 4-0.

CHICAGO. **A. G. SPALDING & BROS.** NEW YORK.

*In the mid 1880's catchers began wearing masks, chest protectors and padded gloves. Here's an early advertisement for baseball equipment.*

*Preceeding page: A view from the stands at St. George's Cricket Field, at a New York Metropolitan home game in the mid 1880's.*

*The New York Giants and the Boston Beaneaters pose for a photo at the start of the '86 National League season.*

usually employed for this purpose (and remained legal until 1893).

In the National League of the 1880s, the Chicago White Stockings were the pre-eminent team; they won the N.L. pennant five out of seven seasons between 1880 and 1886. On the field they were led by manager and first baseman "Cap" Anson, who accumulated over 3000 hits and 1700 RBIs in the 22 years he played major league baseball — a phenomenal feat when you consider that in his prime years the season schedule was less than 100 games.

But as great a player as he was, Anson was constantly being upstaged in the press by another Chicago player, flamboyant outfielder and catcher, Mike "King" Kelly who was baseball's first major superstar. Kelly had perfected the hook slide, and whenever the handsome, hard-playing, hard-drinking Kelly got on base he would be greeted by chants of "Slide Kelly Slide!" from the stands. A popular song of the day went:

*Adrian "Cap" Anson, first baseman and manager of the legendary Chicago White Stockings of the 1880's.*

*Slide, Kelly, slide!*
*Your running's a disgrace!*
*Slide, Kelly, slide!*
*Stay there, hold your base!*
*If someone doesn't steal ya,*
*And your batting doesn't fail ya*
*They'll take you to Australia!*
*Slide, Kelly, slide!*

*Mike "King" Kelly was baseball's first major superstar. Dubbed by the press as "The Ten Thousand Dollar Beauty", chants of "Slide Kelly Slide!" would rise from from the crowd whenever he was on base.*

1. Ryan.
2. Williamson.
3. Farrell.
4. Pfeffer.
5. The Mascot.

Jos. HALL, Photo., Brooklyn, N. Y.

6. Capt. Anson
7. Van Haltren
8. Borchers.
9. Burns.
10. Daly.

CHICAGO BALL CLUB, 1888.

When the charismatic Kelly was sold to Boston after the '86 season for the then-unheard-of sum of $10,000, the news totally shook the baseball world, and the press dubbed him "The Ten Thousand Dollar Beauty" (Kelly himself was to receive $4,000 per year at Boston. He had been making $2,500 per year at Chicago in an age when the average major league ball player was paid about $1,600 per season).

On the mound, the White Stockings were well represented by pitchers: Larry Corcoran, who pitched three no-hitters in the early part of the decade, and John Clarks on who won 53 games for Chicago in the 1885 championship season and then followed up with seasons of 35 and 38 wins. (A year after "King" Kelly was sold to Boston for $10,000, Clarkson was also sold to the same club for $10,000.)

*A Team photo of the Chicago White Stockings in 1888, after "King" Kelly and star pitcher John Clarkson had both been traded away.*

*Opposite: Mike "King" Kelly in a Boston Beaneaters uniform in the late '80's.*

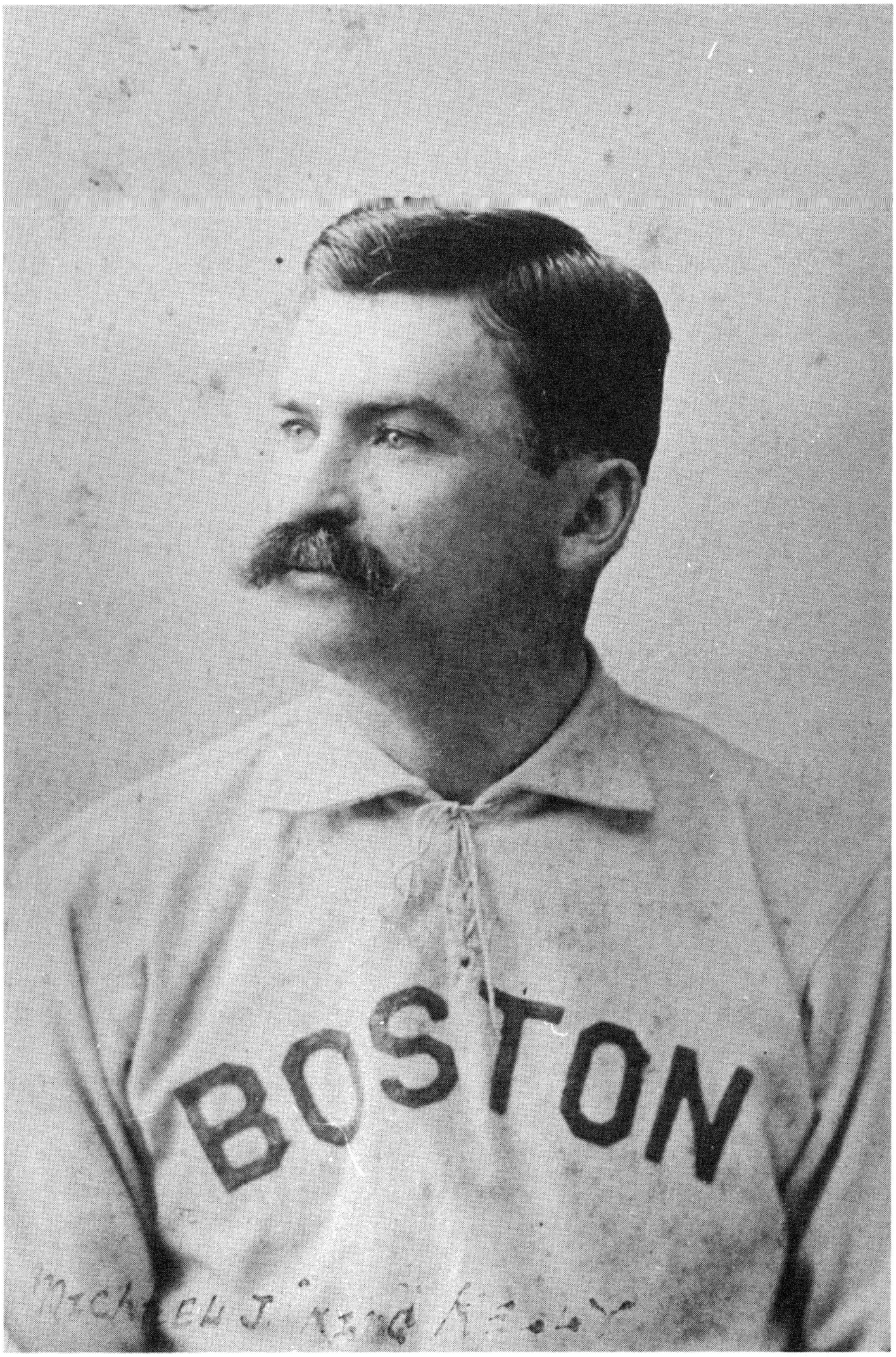
BOSTON

Over in the American Association, the foremost team during this era was the St. Louis Browns, who won four straight Association championships between 1885 and 1888. They were owned by the flamboyant Chris Von der Ahe, a German immigrant who was the proprietor of a beer garden in St. Louis. He had originally gotten into baseball because he saw it as a great opportunity to sell beer (at the St. Louis ball park Von der Ahe's vendors prowled the stands at every game peddling steins of the golden liquid to the thirsty crowd).

Von der Ahe, who was basically ignorant about baseball itself, was nevertheless constantly interfering with the running of the club, much to the chagrin of field manager Charles Commiskey.

Major League Baseball has had a long history of colorful team owners, and Chris Von der Ahe was the very first.

*Below: In the 1880's the foremost team in the American Association was the St. Louis Browns who won four straight Association championships between 1885 and 1888. In this 1888 team photo Charles Commiskey, stands top row, second from right.*

*Opposite: Charles Commiskey. He was the manager and first-baseman of Chris Von der Ahe's St. Louis Browns during the mid-'80's.*

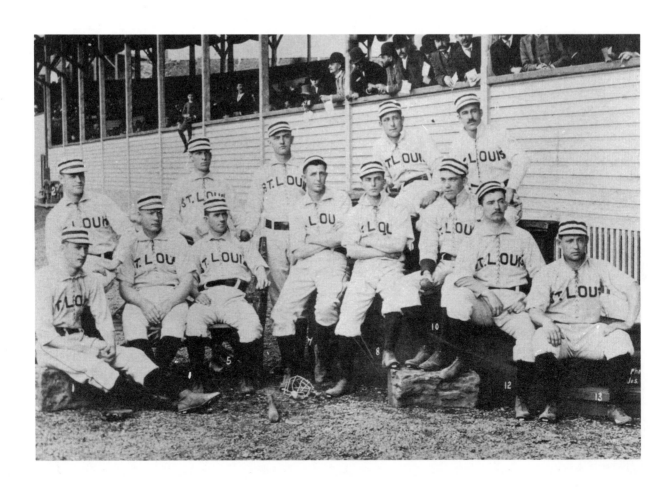

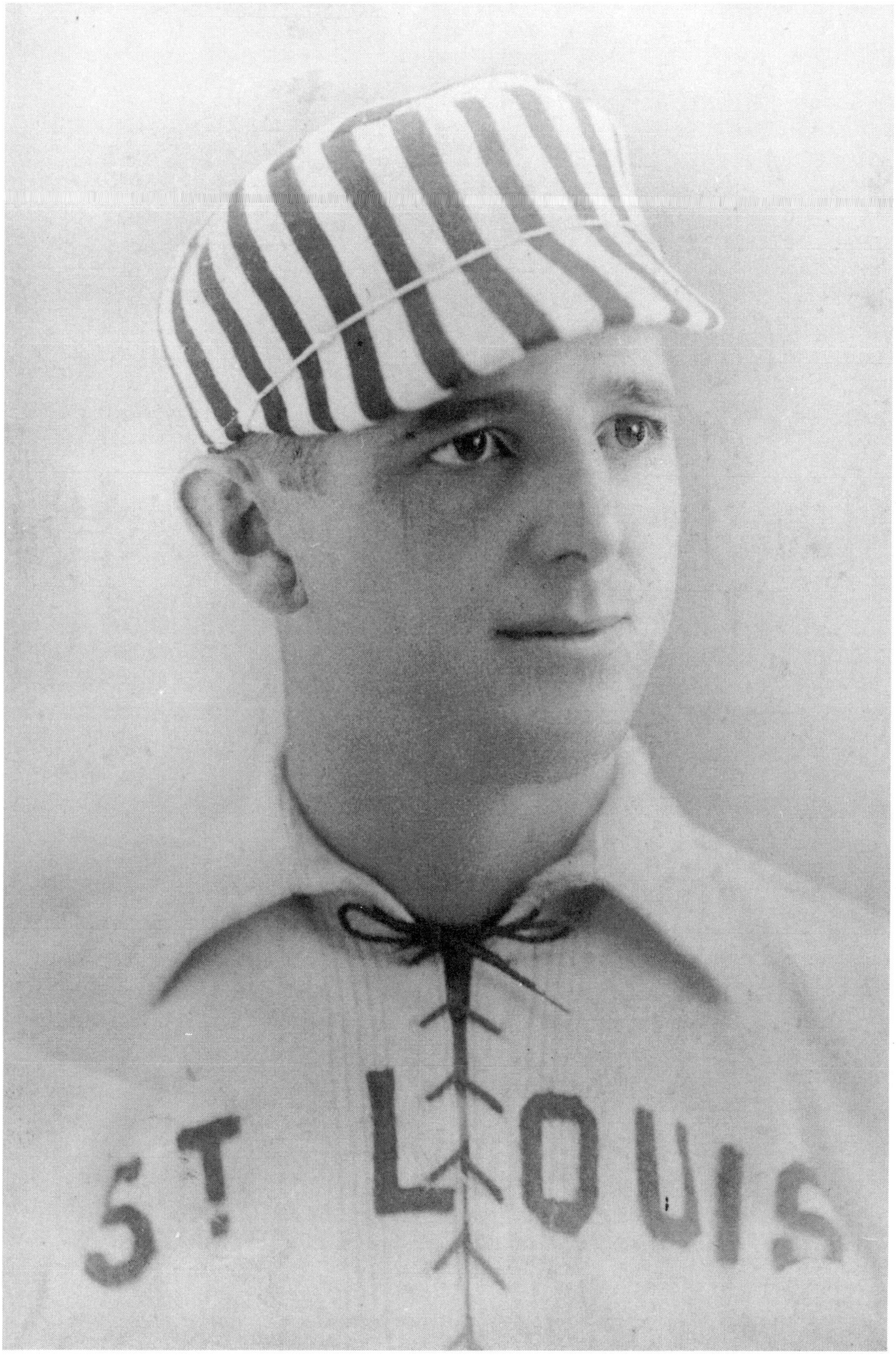
St LOUIS

*Chris Von der Ahe was the very first in Major League Baseball's long history of colorful team owners. In the 1880's, this German immigrant was "der Boss President" of the American Association's St. Louis Browns.*

Such characters as George Steinbrenner, Marge Shott, Charles O. Finley, Bill Veeck and the like, have just been carrying on a tradition that was undoubtedly started by Von der Ahe.

In *Baseball the Early Years*, Harold Seymour says, "Von der Ahe himself could have played in vaudeville. He was a heavy-set man whose face featured a great bulbous nose and a full mustache. He wore loud clothes, spent money liberally, and liked to exclaim 'Nothing is too goot for my poys!'" And when "Der Boss President" was at the ballpark, he "made the players nervous, watching their every move with field glasses, running around the stands blowing a whistle at them, or storming into the dressing room swearing at players whose errors lost the game."

Seymour tells of an incident when Von der Ahe supposedly boasted to a delegation of visitors that he had the biggest baseball diamond in the world. When Commiskey took him aside and whispered that all diamonds were the same size, Von der Ahe promptly retreated and simply claimed that he owned the the biggest infield!

Von der Ahe would ceremoniously take each day's game receipts to the bank in a wheelbarrow, flanked by armed guards, and once he allowed himself to be arrested at the ballpark after he defied a Missouri law which prohibited baseball on Sunday.

Probably his biggest fiasco took place after the 1887 season when Von der Ahe, after being inspired by Chicago's sale of "King" Kelly and John Clarkson to Boston for the then astronomical amount of $10,000 each, decided to fatten his own purse. He promptly decimated his team by selling his top two pitchers, Robert Lee Carruthers and Dave Foutz, along with his number one catcher "Doc" Bushong to Brooklyn for $10,000, and then peddled star outfielder Curt Welch and his only shortstop Bill Gleason to Philadelphia for $5,000.

Unbelievably, Commiskey, starting from almost scratch, was able to recruit enough new players to put together a team for the following year that was was good enough to win the pennant.

Charles Commiskey's exploits as Browns manager and first-baseman are legendary. He is generally credited for revolutionizing the way the position of first base was played. Until he came along, it was customary for all the basemen to stay very near their bases, so when Commiskey ventured out to short right field to catch a fly ball, or else when he would gobble up a hot grounder while playing away from the bag, and then have the pitcher go over to first to cover the play, it changed baseball forever. He was also the first manager to shift his infield in or out, depending on the situation and stage of the game.

On the mound, before they were traded, the Browns were led by pitchers: Bob Caruthers, who won 40 games in '85, and then followed up with seasons of 30 and 29 wins, and Dave Foutz who won 33 games in '85 and then followed up with seasons of 41 and 24 wins. The Browns offence was bolstered by outfielder Tip O'Neill, who hit .435 in 1887 (He was originally credited with a .492 batting average, as walks were counted as hits for that one season).

*Charles "Old Hoss" Radbourn was one of the premier pitchers of the '80's. "Old Hoss" won 60 games in 1884, the year he lead the N.L.'s Providence Grays to victory over the A.A.'s New York Metropolitans in the very first World Series. Radborn spent 12 years in the big leagues and had a lifetime record of 308 wins and 191 losses. He was inducted into the Hall of Fame in 1939.*

# INTOLERANCE

Racism, unfortunately, became an official policy of professional baseball in the 1880s. In 1884, Moses Fleetwood Walker (above) was the first black major league player. He, along with his brother Welday, played in the American Association for the Toledo Blue Stockings, but a stop was soon put to this by the men who ran the game, and no black player was again allowed to compete at a major league level until Jackie Robinson put on a Brooklyn Dodgers uniform in 1947.

New York Base Ball Club. 1888

## MORE COMPETITION

In 1884, another major league was born. It was called the Union Association, but the two established leagues raided enough of the new league's players to put it out of business in one year.

The next league to come along was the Players' League in 1890. It was kind of a slaves revolt, as it was composed of players from the two leagues who were frustrated with limited salaries, unjust fines and the reserve clause (which virtually bound a player to the same team for life). A lack of administrative leadership and heavy gate competition brought about this league's demise after a year.

*The 1888 World Champion New York Giants. Lead by the outstanding pitching of Timothy J. Keefe who won 35 games and lost 12 and lead the league in E.R.A. (1.74) and most strikeouts (333), the Giants took the '88 N.L. pennant with a 84 - 47 record and then went on to defeat the A.A.'s St. Louis Browns in the World Series.*

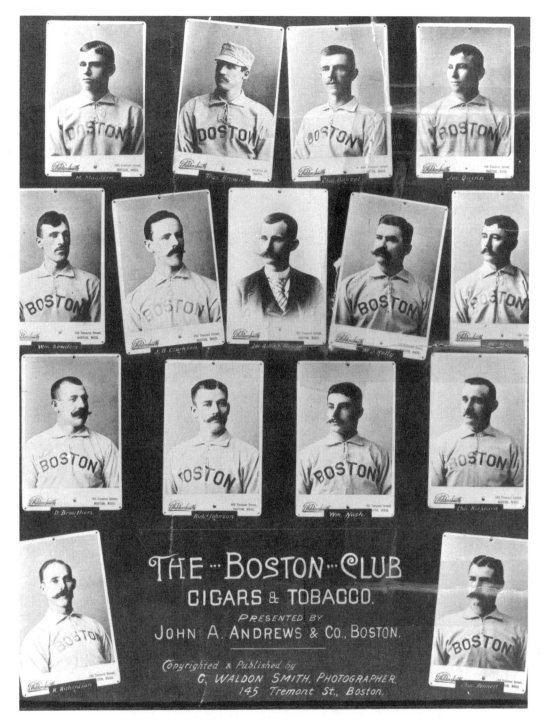

The 1889 Boston Beaneaters as they appeared on tobacco trading cards. There were three future Hall of Famers on this club... Catcher and outfielder Mike "King" Kelly, second row from top, second from right... Pitcher Charles "Old Hoss" Radbourn, third row from top, extreme right... First baseman Dan Brouthers, third row from top, extreme left.

The following year, in 1891 the American Association folded, leaving in its wake a legacy of Sunday games and league control of umpires. Four of its clubs were absorbed by the senior loop, and, for the greater part of the 1890s, a 12-team National League had a monopoly on major league baseball.

# THE BALLPARKS IMPROVE

In the 1880s, the quality and size of ballparks improved somewhat from the rinky-dink structures that were prevalent in the '70s, as baseball attendance grew and major league baseball started to look like it would be around for awhile. The finest ballpark in the land was Lakefront Stadium in Chicago which seated 10,000 spectators, had 18 private boxes, and featured a brass band that played between innings. Towards the end of the decade a 20,000 seat double decker stadium was built in Philadelphia.

*Above: This photo shows the view from the Grand Pavilion of Boston's South End Grounds in the early 1890's. The stadium burned to the ground in 1894.*

*Opposite: The 1890 Boston Reds of the Players League. The Players League lasted for only one year. It was composed of players from the two major leagues who were tired of limited salaries, unjust fines and the reserve clause.*

# THE NATIONAL LEAGUE
# IN THE '90s

At the start of the 1892 season a 12-club N.L. consisted of Cincinnati, Cleveland, St. Louis, Louisville, Chicago and Pittsburgh in the west, and Philadelphia, Brooklyn, Boston, New York, Baltimore and Washington in the east.

On the field, baseball took another major evolutionary step when, in 1893, the pitching distance was changed from 50 feet to the present 60 feet, 6 inches. This put an

GRAND OPENING OF THE NATIONAL LEAGUE BASE BALL SEASON.
At the New Polo Grounds, New York, April 22d, 1891.
THE NEW YORK AND BOSTON BASE BALL CLUBS IN THE FOREGROUND.

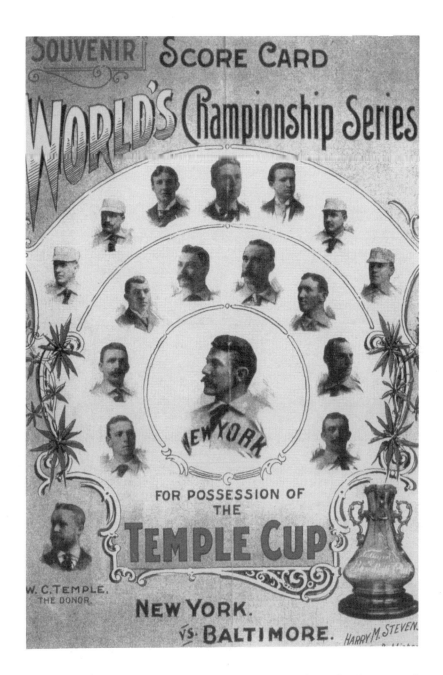

*A poster for the first Temple Cup Championship Series. In the 1890's the National League had a monopoly on major league baseball. Beginning in 1894 the first and second place clubs played each other in a post season series for the Temple Cup.*

*Opposite: 1891 was the last year the National League would face competition from the American Association. On opening day of the N.L. season the New York Giants and the Boston Beaneaters pose for the camera. The Beaneaters would go on to take the pennant that year with a record of 87 wins and 51 losses.*

end to the tremendous advantage the pitchers had enjoyed over the batters (in 1892 the collective batting average for the National League was .245, in '83 (when the distance was increased) it jumped up to .280 and then to .309 the following year).

A post season National League championship series began in 1894. William Temple, owner of the Pittsburgh Pirates donated a trophy, and the first and second place

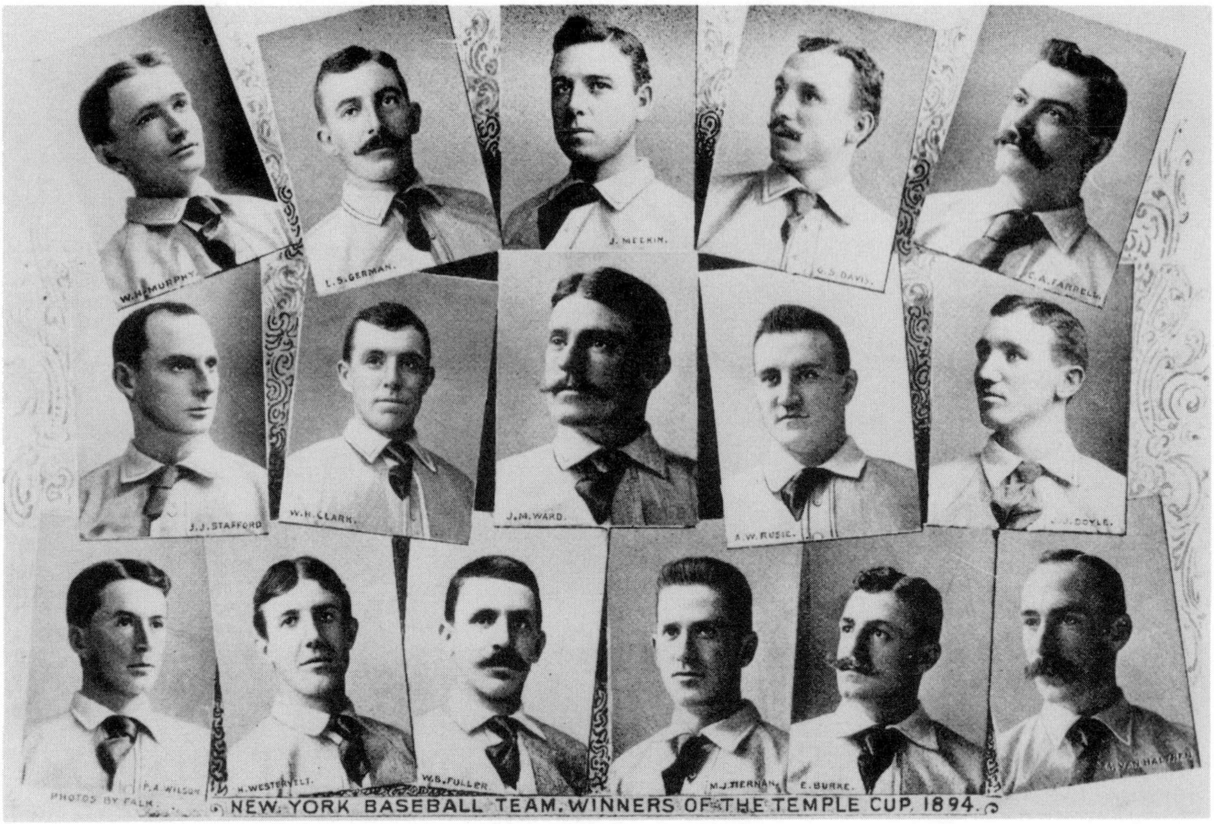
W.H. MURPHY
L.S. GERMAN
J. MEEKIN
C.A. FARRELL
J.J. STAFFORD
W.H. CLARK
J.M. WARD
W.S. FULLER
E. BURKE
NEW YORK BASEBALL TEAM. WINNERS OF THE TEMPLE CUP 1894.

teams played each other for the Temple Cup. The first Temple Cup was won by the New York Giants, who routed the Baltimore Orioles in four straight games.

Those very same Baltimore Orioles were probably the most famous team to come out of this era. The feisty Orioles made baseball into a real team sport, specializing in relays and cut-offs — and pioneering the hit and run. Renowned for the "Old Oriole Spirit" which impelled men to ignore injuries and keep on playing, the gritty Orioles were managed by "Foxy" Ned Hanolon and featured such players as John McGraw and Wee Willie "Hit 'em where they ain't" Keeler. They won three pennants in the 1890s and are known as baseball's *first* "greatest team of all time".

*In 1894 the New York Giants were the winners of the very first Temple Cup series. Although they finished the regular N.L. season in second place, the Giants went on to defeat the first place Baltimore Orioles in four straight games.*

*Opposite: Hall of Fame third baseman Wee Willie "Hit 'em where they ain't" Keeler was a star player for the Orioles in the '90's.*

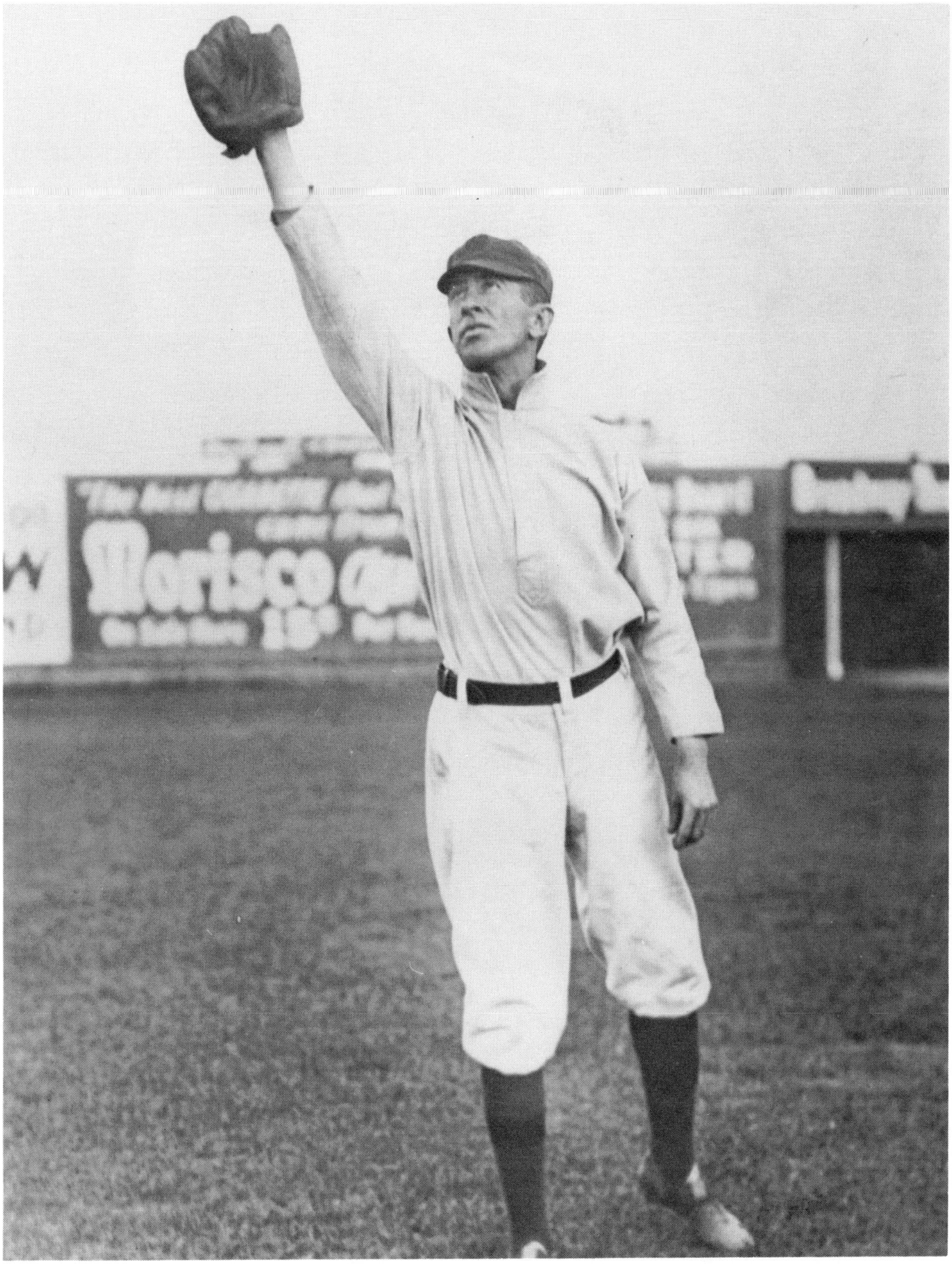
Morisco

*Bancroft "Ban" Johnson was the man responsible for founding the American League.*

*Opposite: This photo depicts all of the players and teams of the 1903 American League.*

## A CHALLENGE FROM THE WEST

It was inevitable that someone else would come along to challenge the National League's supremacy — and that person was a former sportswriter by the name of Ban Johnson. Johnson was the president of the Western League, a minor league that operated in the midwest. He had dreams of someday transforming his circuit into another major league, and in 1900, after the National League dropped four of its 12 franchises, he felt the time was right. So, he changed the name of his circuit to the American League and placed clubs in several eastern cities. Then he snubbed the National Agreement, under which all of organized baseball now operated, and raided the National League for enough talent to give the American League major league status when the season started in 1901.

# HOW COMMISKEY TOOK CHICAGO

Johnson was assisted in his assault on the National League by his good friend and drinking companion Charles Commiskey. Commiskey, whose playing days were now over, had become the owner of the St. Paul Western League franchise, and in 1900 he wanted to move his team into Chicago. Al Spalding, who then owned Chicago's N.L. club, couldn't see anything wrong with a minor league club moving into town, so he let Commiskey have an old

*A middle aged Charles Commiskey. Commiskey (who, due to the shape of his nose, was nicknamed "the Old Roman") founded the Chicago White Sox and helped Ban Johnson start the American League.*

*Overleaf: The first modern day World Series was played in 1903 between the Boston Americans and the Pittsburgh Pirates. At the first game which was played at Boston's Huntington Avenue Base Ball Grounds the crowd floods the field... this was a common occurrence at baseball games played during this era.*

decaying baseball facility by the name of Brotherhood Park under one condition — Commiskey's team could not identify itself as a Chicago club! Commiskey agreed to this provision and then got around it by calling his new club the White Stockings. The National League team (which was then called the Orphans and would soon become the Cubs), had long since stopped calling itself the White Stockings, yet everyone knew it was a name that belonged to Chicago!

Once established in Chicago, Commiskey soon turned his club into a major league operation and eventually built a new ball park for them to play in. In 1904, Commiskey's team became officially known as the *Chicago* White Sox.

# A MAJOR LEAGUE MONOPOLY

A war ensued between the American League and the N.L. for the 1901 and 1902 seasons with many of the senior circuit's top stars jumping ship to the A.L..

In 1903 the National League decided enough was enough, and made peace with the upstart league. The two leagues signed a new National Agreement which gave them both equal status and that October the first modern-day World Series was held with the A.L.'s Boston Americans, led by the pitching of Cy Young and Bill Dinneen, defeating the N.L.'s Pittsburgh Pirates five games to three in a best of nine affair.

In 1904 the two leagues took to squabbling again and no World Series was held. But in 1905 they both kissed and made up and, with the exception of an unsuccessful challenge by the upstart Federal League in 1914 and '15, the two leagues have enjoyed a monopoly on major league baseball ever since.

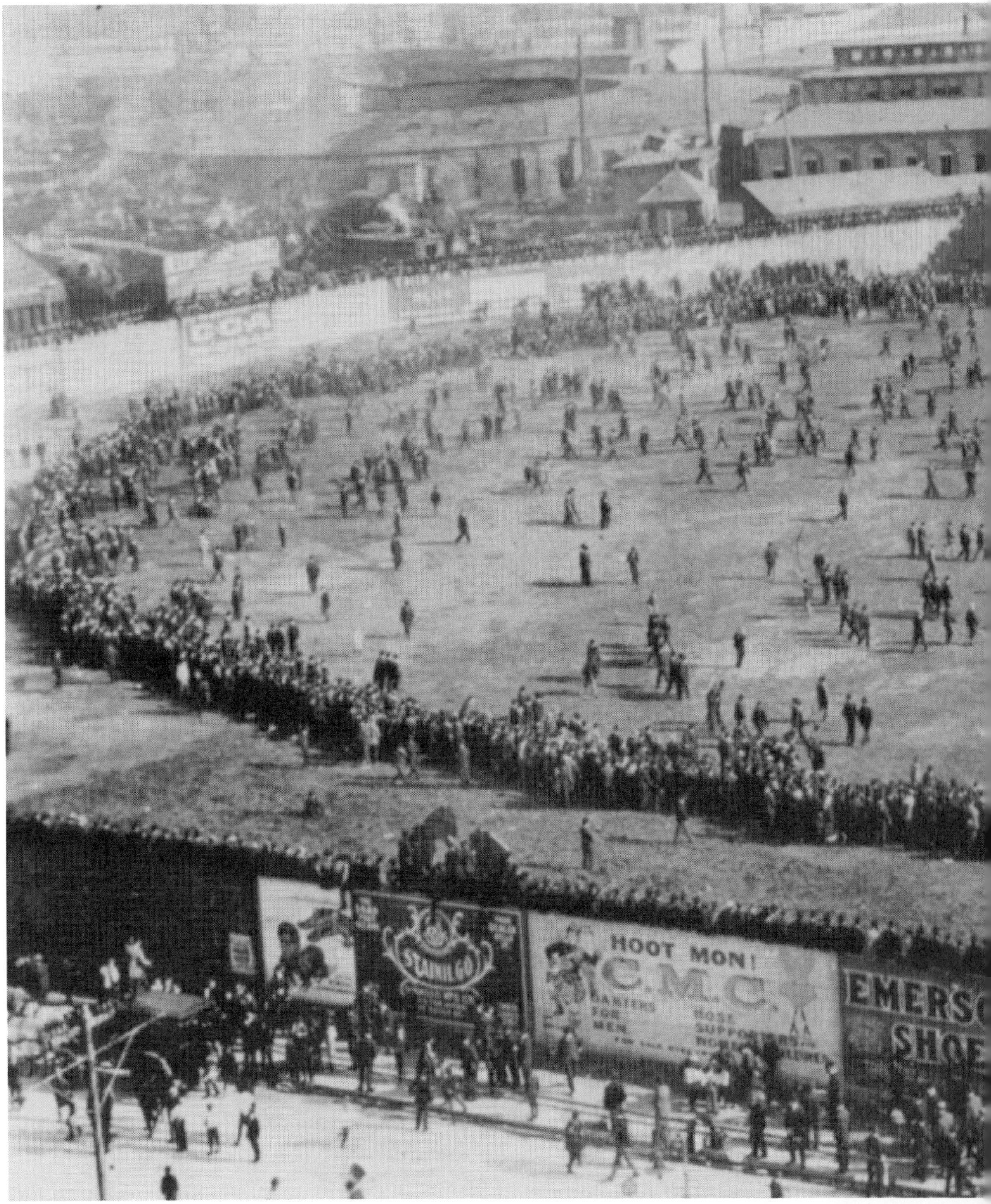
HOOT MON!
C.M.C.

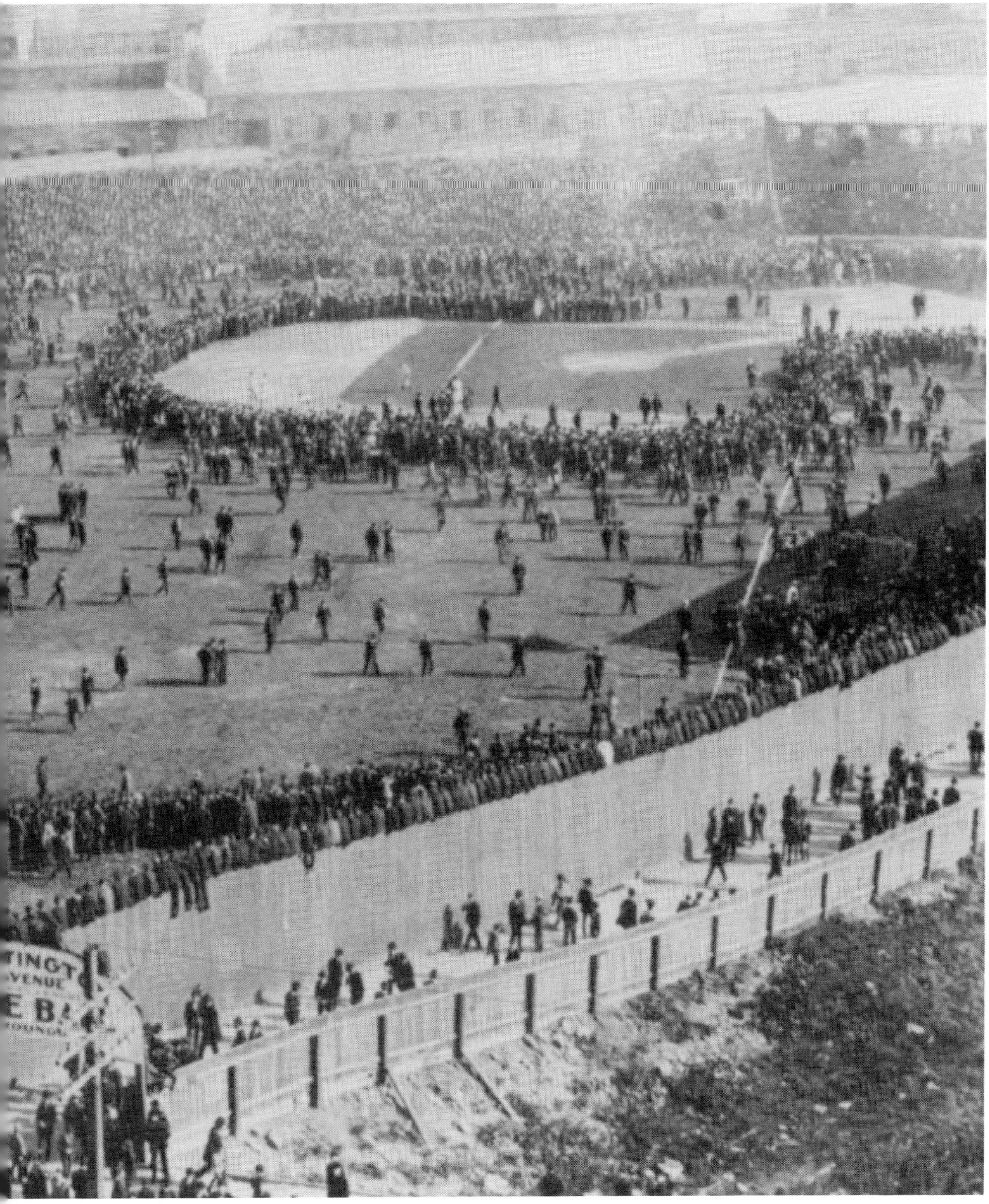

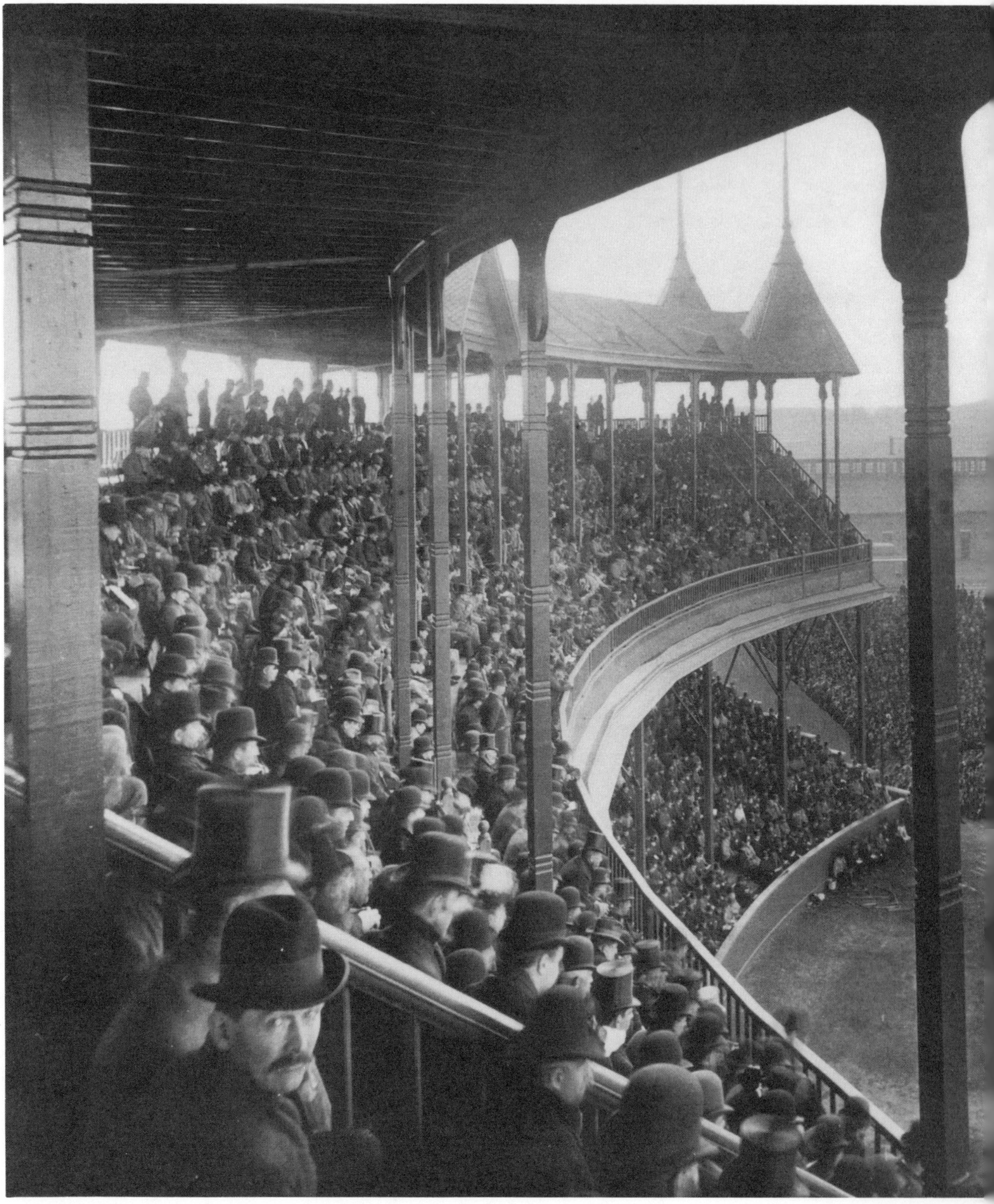

# CHAPTER 5

# A MYTH IS BORN

Our story of the early years of baseball would not be complete without looking into one of the strangest events ever to take place in the long history of the game.

In 1904, Al Spalding, the former major league pitching ace who had since gone on to become a baseball executive and a wealthy manufacturer of sporting equipment, decided that it was demeaning that this great American pastime had found its origin in an English children's game called Rounders. So, the following year, he assembled some like-minded friends, including two U.S. Senators, and had them establish themselves as a commission to look into the origins of baseball — with their ultimate purpose being, if possible, to give it an American ancestry. And that's just what they did!

The commission, which was chaired by former National League president A.G. Mills, had apparently never heard of Alexander Cartwright, or if they did, completely ignored him and declared a deceased American Army General and Civil War hero by the name of Abner Doubleday to be the inventor of baseball. Unfortunately, the commission had no real evidence to support this conclusion. As a matter of fact, there has never been any real evidence that Doubleday had much, if anything, to do with baseball.

The commission based their findings on a letter they had received from an elderly man by the name of Abner Graves who claimed to have been a boyhood friend of Doubleday's.

Graves, a mining engineer from Colorado who was well into his 80s, stated in his letter that sometime around 1839 (as he put it, "either the spring prior to or following the 'Log Cabin and Hard Cider' campaign of General William H. Harrison for the presidency"), he had seen Doubleday directing some 20 to 50 boys around in a Cooperstown, N.Y. school yard while they were playing a game of Town Ball, which was a form of Rounders. Because, as Graves claimed, Doubleday had the boys form themselves into teams with *eleven* players on each side, and four bases had been used in the game, Graves was convinced that he had been witnessing the actual invention of baseball.

The facts themselves tended to nullify Graves' claim: the game Graves described involved the practice of "soaking" runners, or throwing the ball at them to get an out; Town Ball had been played in North America for at least seventy-five years prior to 1839, sometimes with definite sides or teams, and sometimes with just one player against the whole school yard, using *any number* of bases; and furthermore, Doubleday *never* in his whole life had been known to even utter the word baseball. Apparently this made no difference to the commission. They accepted Graves' story and, in 1907, declared Abner Doubleday the game's inventor.

Doubleday, the heroic Civil War hero, had turned out to be a convenient figurehead for the commission, in their quest to give the game an all-American heritage.

*Albert Goodwill Spalding, the major league pitching ace who went on to become a successful baseball executive and manufacturer of sporting equipment. He tried to create his own history of baseball by promoting the Doubleday myth.*

# AL SPALDING — THE MAN BEHIND THE DOUBLEDAY MYTH

It's time we took a closer look a man whose name has cropped up throughout this book, a man who has contributed greatly to the history of baseball, though there are those who might not consider all of his contributions to be positive.

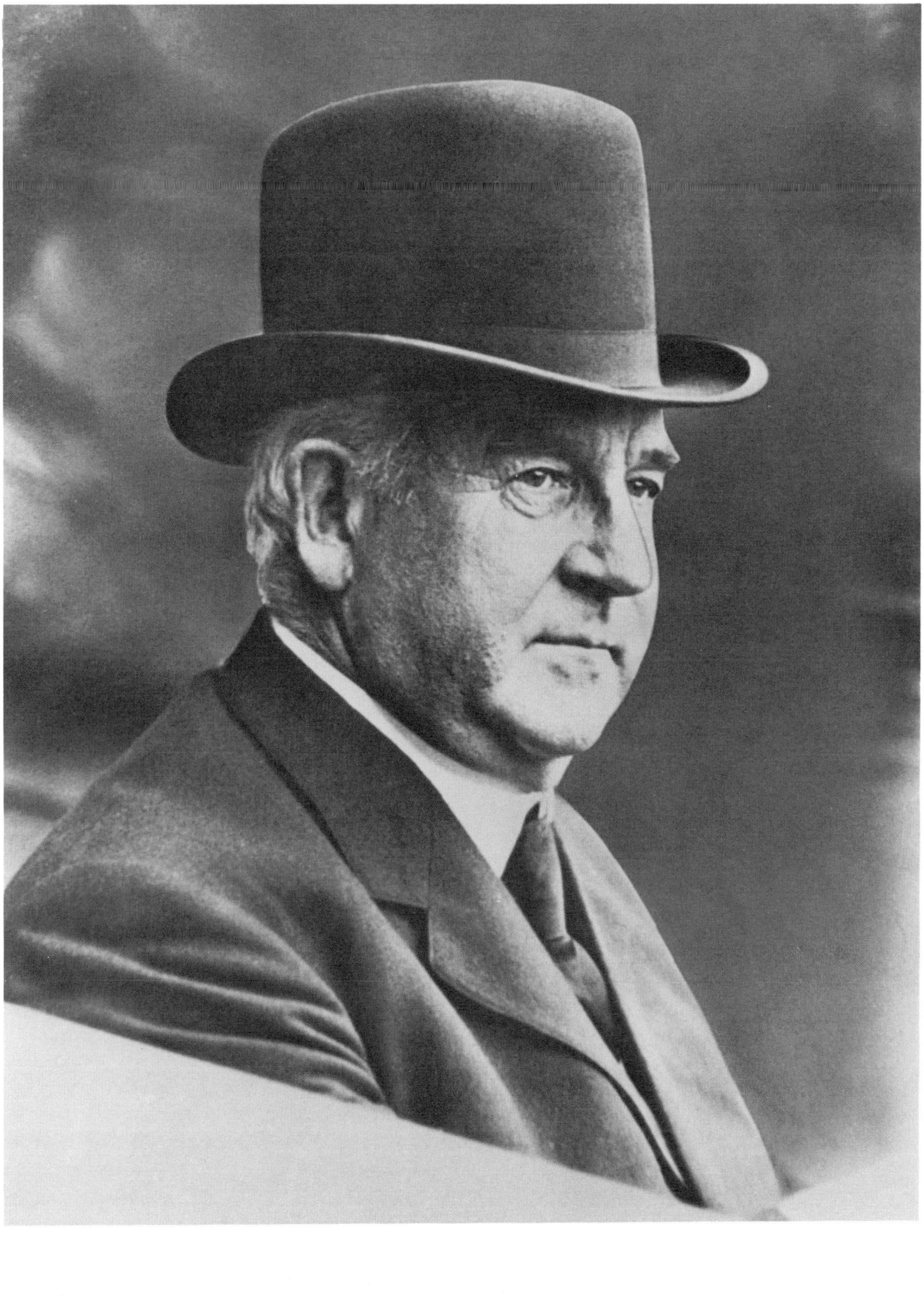

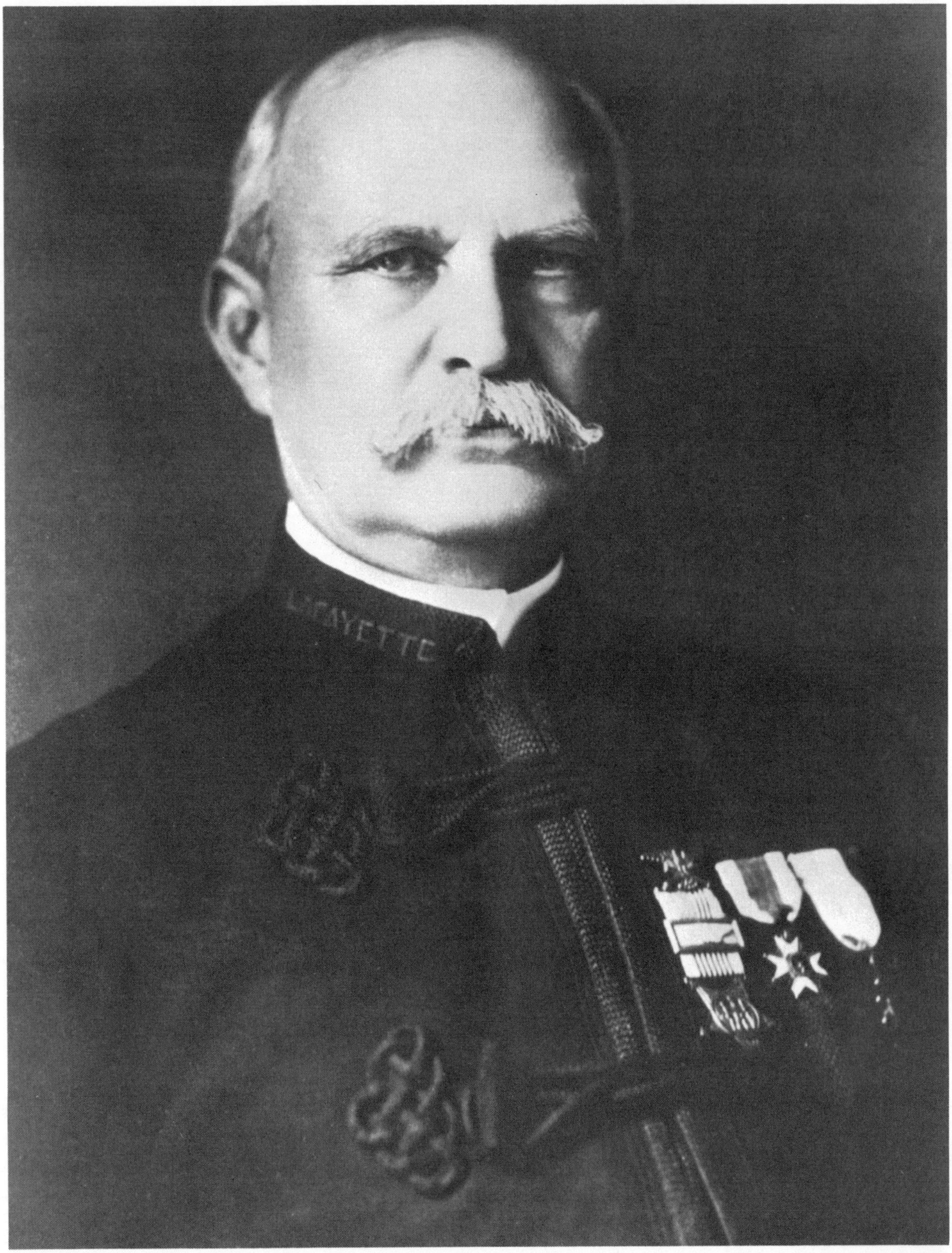

It could be said of Al Spalding that he never met an opportunity to make money out of baseball that he didn't like. Born in Byron, Illinois in 1850, Albert Goodwill Spalding grew up to become a star pitcher in baseball's first professional league, the National Association. From 1871 to 1875, pitching for the Boston Red Stockings he won 207 games and lost only 56 . . . *an average of 41 wins per season!*

When the National League came into being, Spalding initially managed the Chicago club, and then went on to become an executive with the team and then eventually owner of the franchise. He was one of baseball's great entrepreneurs. In 1876, along with his brother and brother-in-law, he established the firm of A.G. Spalding and Brothers, which started out as a sporting goods store in Chicago and then evolved into a major manufacturer of sporting goods.

Spalding had no qualms about using his influence as a baseball executive to promote his business — among other things, he gave the National League free baseballs, and even paid them a dollar for each dozen they used, in turn for the league designating his ball as the "official" ball of the league. This, of course, helped to create a great demand for Spalding baseballs by the public.

He also became the publisher of the *Official League Book,* which carried league rules, and additionally he published *Spalding's Official Base-Ball Guide,* an annual collection of team and individual records which was known to feature articles which pushed Spalding's viewpoint on many baseball issues — and helped to sell massive amounts of Spalding sporting equipment.

As a baseball executive, he helped to work out the territorial scheme that kept clubs from competing with each other for the same fans, and was instrumental in breaking up the Player's Brotherhood, which had called for the first players' strike in 1890.

Al Spalding organized the Great World Baseball Tour of 1888-89, where he took his Chicago club and players

*Former National League President A.G. Mills was the chairman of the so called "commission" that named Abner Doubleday as the inventor of baseball.*

from other teams on a tour around the world in order to promote the great American game of baseball. On the six-month junket they visited such places as Australia, Ceylon, Egypt, Italy, France and Britain. They played some 42 games before an estimated 200,000 people, and the game itself generally received mixed reviews. After witnessing a baseball exhibition at London's Kensington Oval, Britain's Prince of Wales stated that baseball was "an excellent game", although he considered cricket to be "superior."

Spalding partially retired from baseball in 1901, when

*Hall of Fame member Henry Chadwick was the first full-time baseball writer and the inventor of the box score.*

he moved to California, joined a religious cult and eventually made an unsuccessful run for U.S. Senate. He died in Point Loma, California in 1915.

But it is an incident that began in 1905 that we shall concern ourselves with right now, for it was then that Al Spalding actually tried to re-write baseball history to suit his own particular viewpoint.

In an 1903 essay, writer Henry Chadwick had declared baseball to be an offshoot of the British children's game of Rounders. This outraged Spalding who, as Spalding biographer Peter Levene puts it, had become "convinced that a game so fundamentally representative of American values had to be American in origin."

The writer of this "blasphemy", Henry Chadwick, was himself an important early baseball figure. The British-born Chadwick, who as a teenager had immigrated to the U.S. along with his family, had seen his first baseball game in 1848 at Elysian Fields and immediately fell in love with the game. He then devoted his life to writing about, and promoting, baseball.

Throughout the years Chadwick wrote about baseball in such publications as the New York *Clipper*, the New York *Herald* and the Brooklyn *Eagle*, and he explained the game and its techniques in his own *Base Ball Manual*, *Beadle's Dime Base-Ball Player* and *De Witt's Base-Ball Guide*. Ironically, he also edited *Spalding's Official Base-Ball Guide* from 1879 to 1908.

Henry Chadwick is acknowledged to be the first full-time baseball writer, and is credited as being the inventor of the box score. Chadwick, who sometimes is referred to as "the Father of Baseball", was inducted into the National Baseball Hall of Fame in 1938.

In other words, Chadwick was a very creditable source, but that all-American chauvinist, Al Spalding, nevertheless set out to prove him wrong — and in doing so, Spalding set the wheels in motion for what has turned out to be baseball's longest running scandal: the Cartwright - Doubleday controversy.

# A COMMISSION . . .
# IN NAME ONLY

In 1905, acting on his own authority, Spalding put together his commission to investigate the origin of baseball. It had no official status of any kind, and Spalding remained behind the scenes, pulling all the strings.

The commission was composed of James Sullivan, the president of the Amateur Athletic Union and a Spalding employee, who acted as secretary; former players George Wright and Al Reach, who, like Spalding, were both in the sporting goods manufacturing business, ostensibly in competition with Spalding, yet he secretly partially owned both their companies (Wright, by the way, as Cartwright biographer Harold Peterson points out, could quite likely have set the commission straight, as he actually played against the Knickerbockers in the 1860s and obviously had been aquatinted with some of the older men who had known and played with Cartwright, but Wright never attended a single meeting); former baseball executive and U.S. Senator Arthur P. Gorman; and three former National League Presidents, Nicholas E. Young, Senator Morgan E. Bulkeley, and A.G. Mills, who chaired the commission.

In the three years that the commission existed, no genuine research was ever done. Sullivan collected a couple of hundred letters that were sent in from all over the land, and finally accepted the letter from Graves (which had been handed to him by Spalding) as the best obtainable evidence as to the origin of the game.

# DON'T BLAME DOUBLEDAY!

*Abner Doubleday, the distinguished Civil War hero who never, ever in his whole life had anything to do with baseball, but was nevertheless named as the game's inventor.*

Just who was Abner Doubleday anyway?  Well, he was born in Ballson Spa, N.Y. in 1819, went to school in Auburn, N.Y. and then entered the West Point Military Academy in 1839.  In a notable military career, Doubleday rose to the rank of General during the Civil War and is credited with firing the first Union shot in defence of Fort Sumter. He then went on to distinguish himself in battles at Bull Run, Antietam and Gettysburg.

Not only is he *not known* to have ever played baseball, Doubleday, who was also an excellent writer and public

speaker, never made a single reference to the game in all of his writings and speeches. Furthermore, after he died all of his diaries were examined and there was no mention of baseball was found there either.

More importantly, Doubleday *never claimed* to have invented baseball. He died in 1893, some 14 years before Spalding's commission came to their remarkable conclusion, and he certainly wasn't around to refute their findings.

As Harold Peterson so aptly puts it: "Abner Doubleday didn't invent baseball. Baseball invented Abner Doubleday."

## A HALL OF FAME FOUNDED ON A MYTH

When the Mills Commission published their findings in 1907, it, of course, made headlines in newspapers all across the land, and the Doubleday story was soon accepted by sportswriters and the general public as being the truth.

The Doubleday myth persisted until the mid-1930s when, due to a remarkable series of events, it was finally shot down.

In 1936, construction was underway in the small village of Cooperstown N.Y. for a building which would house a National Baseball Hall of Fame. It was to open in 1939 as part of a celebration to mark the centennial of Abner Doubleday's alleged invention of the game, right there in Cooperstown, 100 years earlier.

The man behind the Hall of Fame was Stephen C. Clark, a wealthy Cooperstown resident and Doubleday myth-believer, who, in this monumental endeavor, had obtained the support and cooperation of such baseball notables as Ford Frick, then president of the National League, Baseball Commissioner Kenesaw Mountain Landis, and American League President William Harridge.

A few years earlier Clark had established a small base-

*On June 12, 1939, some four thousand baseball fans showed up for the opening of the National Baseball Hall of Fame in Cooperstown N.Y.. The opening ceremonies were held in conjunction with so called "centennial" of the birth of baseball.*

ball museum in Cooperstown. In the museum, along with other early baseball artifacts, was an old homemade baseball that had been found in an attic trunk in a nearby village. The ball was believed to have once belonged to Abner Graves. It was therefore assumed that Doubleday himself must have at some time actually touched the "magic" ball . . . and therefore, it became known as the "Doubleday baseball".

It was also in 1936, three years before they actually had a building, that the Hall of Fame began inducting baseball greats. Ty Cobb, Babe Ruth, Honus Wagner, Christy Mathewson and Walter Johnson were the first to be honored.

Things were looking just great in Cooperstown for the

*The 1939 opening of the Hall of Fame was attended by some of baseball's all time greats. Here, some of the Hall of Fame's early inductees assemble for a group portrait. This incredible gathering of baseball talent consists of: Top row - left to right - Honus Wagner, Grover Cleveland Alexander, Tris Speaker, Napoleon Lajoie, George Sisler, Walter Johnson. Bottom row - left to right - Eddie Collins, George Herman "Babe" Ruth, Connie Mack, Cy Young.*

forthcoming combined opening of the new building and commemoration of baseball's "centennial". An elaborate celebration had been proposed for the summer of 1939. A pageant portraying baseball's historical highlights was planned, and an all-star game between some of baseball's all-time great players was to be held. The State of New York had declared Cooperstown to be "the birthplace of baseball" and had helped to publicize the event by printing pamphlets and putting up road signs to that effect. The U.S. Government got into the act by issuing a special postage stamp to commemorate the event.

But then a funny thing happened on the way to the Centennial celebration . . .

When news of the forthcoming festivities got out, it caused quite a stir among baseball historians, a number of whom began to publicly declare that the Doubleday story was nothing but pure baloney. The most notable of these baseball scholars was Robert W. Henderson of the New York Public Library who immediately published irrefutable evidence that baseball had indeed been derived from Rounders.

Meanwhile in far off Hawaii, Alexander Cartwright's grandson Bruce heard about the planned celebration. He knew enough about his late ancestor's achievements to fire off a letter to the centennial organizers explaining his grandfather's role in the development of the game.

The centennial organizers researched Cartwright's claim and its legitimacy soon became apparent. As a result, Alexander Cartwright was inducted into the National Baseball Hall of Fame in 1938 for his contributions to the development of the game. Abner Doubleday, on the other hand, has *never* been inducted into the Hall of Fame.

The Cartwright revelation did not stop the impending Centennial ceremonies though; over $100,000 had already been invested, so the organizers just toned things down a bit and, in June of 1939, went ahead and held the festivities anyway!

# IN COOPERSTOWN . . . THE MYTH LIVES ON

The Doubleday myth is still alive and well in the small friendly village of Cooperstown, where the local merchants do their best to cash in on the three-to four-hundred thousand visitors who flock there each year to visit the Hall of Fame.

Ever since its opening, the Hall of Fame, unfortunately, has done very little to tell the real story of the origin of baseball and to discredit the Doubleday fable . As a matter of fact they have, in a mild way, always promoted the Doubleday story, and still do today. In the Hall of Fame they have traditionally maintained a display that glorifies Abner Doubleday and focuses on the Mills Commission findings, and each year they put out an official publication that promotes Doubleday's alleged baseball achievements and makes mention of the magical "Doubleday baseball" — but then they conclude their findings with a copout, stating that if baseball didn't actually originate in Cooperstown in 1839, it probably originated "in a similar rural atmosphere" and therefore Cooperstown is "certainly an acceptable symbolic site."

The reason the Hall of Fame tap-dances around the Doubleday myth is apparently financial. They seem to believe that the Doubleday fable helps to attract people to Cooperstown. Yet, if they were to publicly totally denounce the Doubleday story, and proclaim Alexander Cartwright as the true founder of baseball, would it really hurt business? After more than 50 years in one location it seems unlikely.

Baseball fans would still flock to the Hall of Fame to see the exhibits and pay homage to their favorite players. But the folks that run Cooperstown seem to think that the truth might somehow kill the goose that laid the golden egg.

The Hall of Fame is a fine institution that does many great things for the game of baseball, and if the perpetua-

*This poster was issued to promote the 1939 opening of the National Baseball Hall of Fame and baseball's so called "centennial".*

tion of the myth didn't have any real consequences, then who would care? But unfortunately, as long as this nonsense continues, Alexander Cartwright, the true founder of baseball, will never be given the proper honor and recognition that he deserves in the baseball world, and baseball fans everywhere will ultimately lose out by being kept in ignorance of the true history and origin of *their* game.

# THE SOUND OF SILENCE

And where does Major League Baseball (the multi-billion dollar organization that represents all of the major league clubs) stand on all this? Have they done anything to glorify and promote Baseball's true early history? Do they hold an annual Cartwright day in honor of the founder of the game that they have made millions upon millions of dollars out of? Do they insist that statues of Alexander Cartwright be erected at their ballparks? Do they present the winner of the World Series with a Cartwright trophy? No, they do none of this. They have been almost totally silent on the subject over the years and the reason is rather obvious: it's in their best interest to stay on good terms with the folks that run the Hall of Fame.

This is because the Hall of Fame is a great promotional device for Major League Baseball. Not only are the greatest players ever to play in the big leagues enshrined in the Hall of Fame, but each summer a gigantic ceremony is held in Cooperstown where the big shots of Major League Baseball and the Hall of Fame all get together, along with thousands of fans, for the induction of newly elected members.

These festivities are usually followed, on the next day, by an exhibition baseball game between two major league clubs at — yes, you guessed it — Doubleday Field, which is a 10,000 seat stadium located in the center of Cooperstown that supposedly stands on the spot where Abner Doubleday allegedly invented the game.

Between the Hall of Fame and Major League Baseball, the sound of silence on the the subject of the true origin of the game of baseball is truly deafening.

Overlooked and forgotten in this whole mess, is Alexander Cartwright Jr., the man who first drew up the original rules for the great game of baseball. What did he do, if anything, to deserve such a fate? Well, if he hadn't vanished from the North American baseball scene only a few years after he gave us the game, maybe things would be different. You'll learn of his fate in the next chapter.

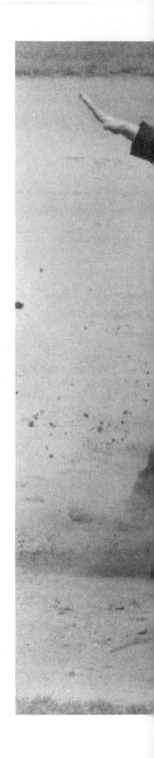

*Baseball has come a long way from when it first appeared in North America as a game with no fixed rules that was played by children in cow pastures, to the multi-billion dollar spectacle that is now part of our lives.*

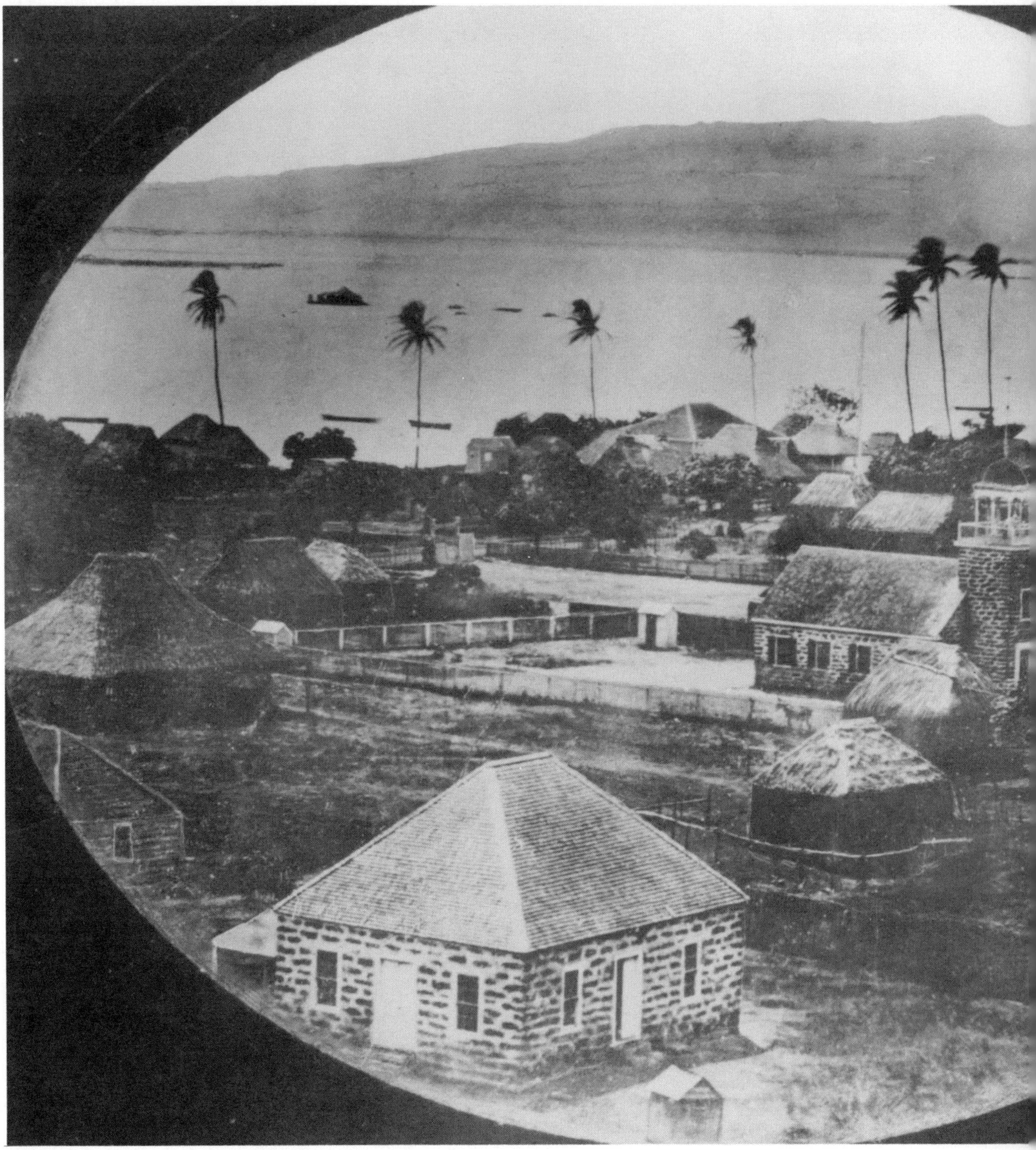

*Honolulu in the mid-1800's*

# CHAPTER 6

# CARTWRIGHT GOES HAWAIIAN

As was pointed out in Chapter 3 of this book, within the span of mere two and a half decades after Alexander Cartwright Jr. introduced baseball to the world, at Elysian Fields in Hoboken New Jersey, on June 19, 1846, the new game had spread like wildfire all across the North American continent. People had begun playing it in small towns and large cities everywhere, and the first professional league had been formed in 1871 . . . exactly 25 years later.

Yet Alexander Cartwright was not around to witness how popular this little game of his would become.

After that historic summer of 1846, Cartwright spent only three more years in the New York City area with his Knickerbocker club. On March 1, 1849 after bidding goodby to his wife Eliza and their four children, and promising to send for them, he joined up with a group of friends and set out on a journey to the California goldfields.

They travelled by land, first by rail to Pittsburgh, and then by covered wagon the rest of the way. The trip took 156 days, and Cartwright, according to his diaries, walked most of the way.

He took a few balls and bats along with him on the excursion, and became kind of a baseball Johnny Appleseed, planting the seeds of the game across the land. At many of their rest stops Cartwright and his party spent their leisure time playing baseball. He is said to have taught the game to miners, storekeepers, Indians and white settlers at frontier towns and Army posts all along the way.

*Alexander Cartwright in Honolulu during the 1880's. Besides virtually inventing the game of baseball, Cartwright's other achievements include founding the Honolulu fire department. Here, he poses with his Chief's hat on.*

*Somewhere out west in 1849, Alexander Cartwright and his friends play baseball at a wagon train rest stop.*

Upon arriving at the California goldfields in August, Cartwright decided that it was too crowded to suit him and he immediately went to San Francisco were he met up with his brother Alfred DeForest Cartwright, who had come there by ship all the way around Cape Horn.

After spending only five days in San Francisco, Alexander decided to go even more westward and he jumped aboard a Peruvian sailing ship by the name of Pacifico which was heading for the Sandwich Islands (which were later to become Hawaii).

And that's were Alexander Cartwright spent the rest of his life — in the tropical paradise of the Hawaiian Islands.

He became a successful businessman and one of Honolulu's leading citizens. Among other things, he founded the Honolulu fire department and served as its chief for nine years. Eventually he even became a friend and financial advisor to the Hawaiian royal family.

The jolly, gregarious Cartwright spent his leisure hours teaching baseball, not only to his own sons (his family had joined him soon after he arrived), but also to the people of Hawaii — and baseball soon became the most popular pastime in Honolulu, long before it grew into the national game on the mainland.

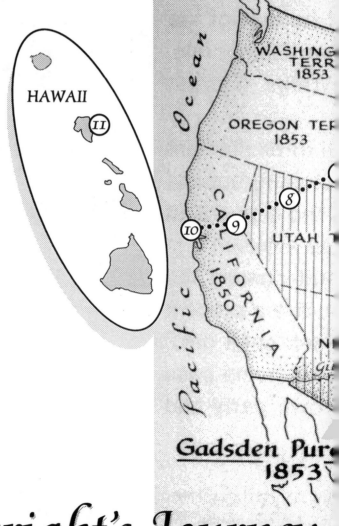

1. *Left New York City March 1*

2. *Pittsburgh (PA) March 3*

3. *St. Louis (MO) April 11*

4. *Independence (MO) April 20*

5. *Fort Kearney (NE) May 10*

6. *Fort Laramie (WY) May 25*

7. *Fort Hall (ID) June 25*

8. *Passed near Winnemucca (NV) July 14*

9. *California Goldfields August 4*

10. *Left San Franciso August 15*

11. *Arrived Oahu August 28*

*Cartwright's Journey*

Alexander Cartwright died in Honolulu in 1892, at the age of 72. He is well remembered in Hawaii, as the man who brought baseball to the islands. In Honolulu there is a Cartwright Street and a small ballpark called Cartwright Field, both named in his honor, and a bronze plaque dedicated to him hangs at City Hall.

It is said that in 1939, when Babe Ruth was visiting Honolulu, he placed flower leis on Cartwright's grave.

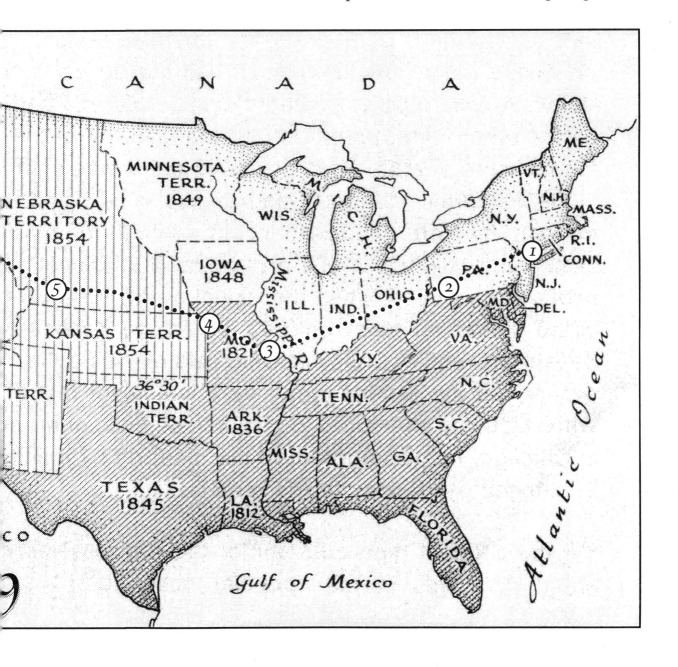

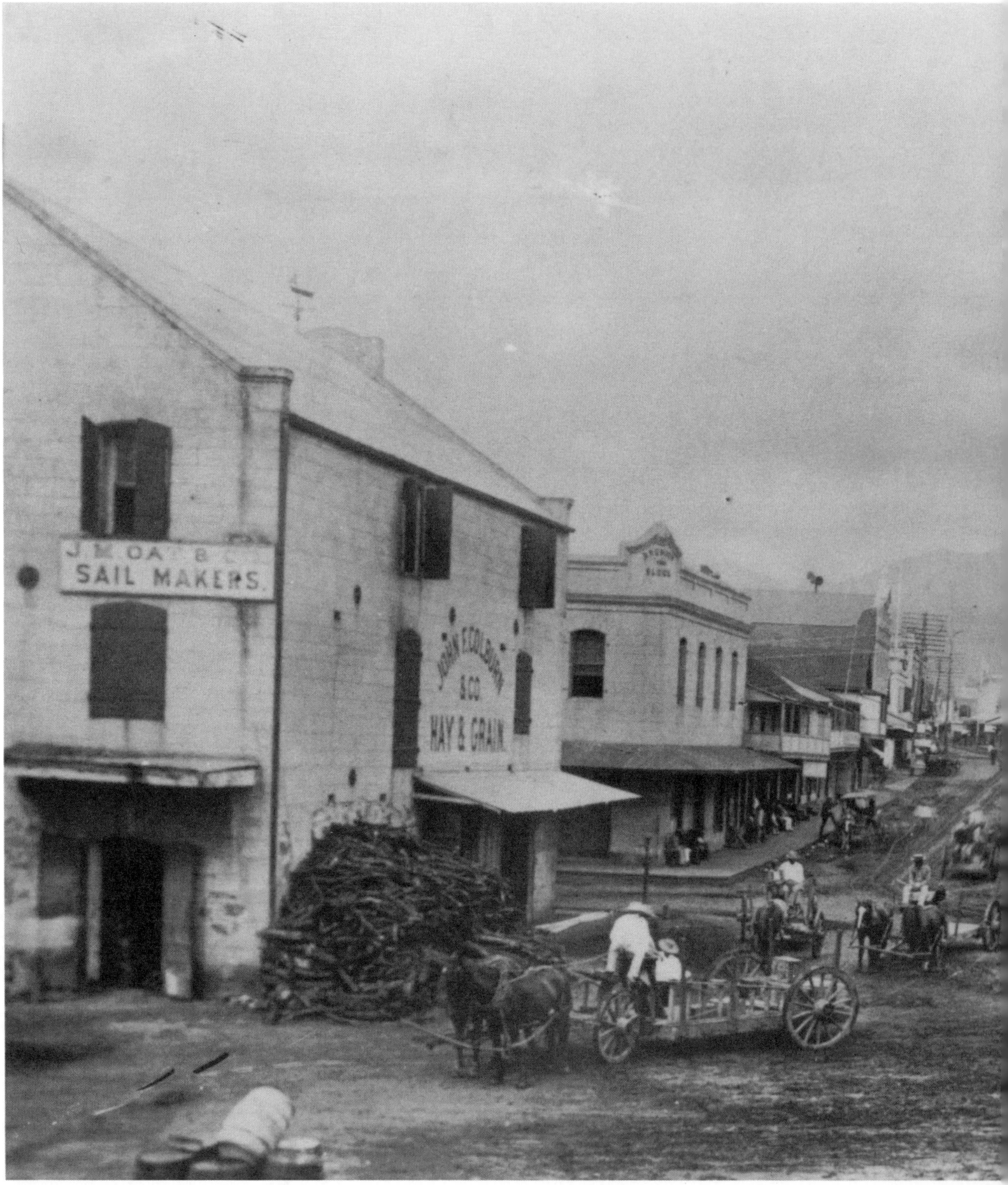
SAIL MAKERS.
HAY & GRAIN.

*This is what Honolulu looked like in the 1850's when Alexander Cartwright settled there.*

# CHAPTER SEVEN

# MODERN DAY EFFORTS TO HONOR CARTWRIGHT

Fortunately for those of us who appreciate the true history of baseball, Alexander Cartwright Jr. has not been completely forgotten in this day and age. Here is a story of recent efforts that have been made to honor Cartwright and his achievements.

New Jersey attorney Stephen Speiser is a man on a mission. Since 1989, he's been leading a campaign to establish a new baseball museum and monument to honor Alexander Cartwright in Hoboken, New Jersey, which is the location where Elysian Fields once existed. He has also been behind efforts to have the U.S. Congress formally declare June 19 as a National Baseball Day — for, as was pointed out earlier in this book, it was on June 19, 1846 that Alexander Cartwright first introduced the game of baseball to the world at Elysian Fields in Hoboken.

Speiser would like to establish his "American Baseball Heritage Museum" in the northern end of Hoboken, not far from the Hudson River, on the exact spot where Elysian Fields once flourished. As of the publication of this book, on this site there now sits an abandoned, decaying coffee factory, and beside it there is a small playground called Elysian Park.

Speiser would like to see Elysian Fields (at least partially) restored to its former glory. Not only did Cartwright introduce baseball here, but all of the great early teams played here — the Atlantic, Excelsior and Eckford clubs of Brooklyn, the Gotham, Eagle, Empire and Mutual clubs of

*Opposite page: New Jersey attorney Stephen Speiser stands in front of the abandoned coffee factory that now occupies most of the area where Elysian Fields was once located.*

New York, as well as the Knickerbockers themselves, all came over by ferry from Manhattan and made the mile long hike from the ferry docks to the five acres of meadowlands that were then known as Elysian Fields. In the 1840s, '50s and '60s, Elysian Fields was a baseball mecca, and is truly one of the great historic locations of the game and deserves to be honored as such. "It's sad to see

*In Hoboken this decaying, abandoned coffee factory now sits on the spot where Elysian Fields once flourished.*

what's become of this area," says Speiser, who started organizing annual Baseball Day celebrations in Hoboken in 1990.

The Baseball Day events, which are usually held each June 19, are designed to show the world that Hoboken, not Cooperstown, is truly the birthplace of baseball. They have consisted of such things as parades through downtown Hoboken; various ceremonies attended by such New Jersey politicians as the mayor of Hoboken and the Governor of the state; little league games; sports memorabilia auctions; celebrity softball games; fireworks, and, of course, recreations of early baseball games. At one such event they even had a recreation ferry ride where two teams dressed in mid-1800s clothing were brought across the Hudson River from Manhattan to Hoboken, then made the mile-long walk to Elysian Fields and held an old time baseball game at a nearby college ball field.

Former Major Leaguers such as Bobby Thompson, Bud Harrelson, Roy White, Ed Kranepool, along with broadcaster Dick Schaap, have all attended the Hoboken festivities. And twice, Speiser has even flown Alexander Cartwright IV out from Seattle to attend the ceremonies. He is, after all, the great-great-grandson of the father of baseball.

And what kind of a person is Stephen Speiser? Is this genial, outgoing native of New York City some kind of a baseball nut? Some kind of a baseball history fanatic? No, not at all; he would consider himself "a normal male, with a normal interest in baseball," who, like most of us "grew up with the Doubleday - Cooperstown myth." When he moved his law practice to Hoboken in the mid '80s, he discovered the truth about the birth of baseball and, ever since, has been on a crusade to right what he sees as a horrible wrong.

But it hasn't been easy. He's been battling both the national press and the Cooperstown hierarchy: As for the press, "the media just doesn't seem to give a damn," said a rather disillusioned sounding Speiser recently. "I've been

trying to get my message out for years, but the press seems to be incapable of giving this subject the thoughtful, measured analysis that it deserves. All they're interested in is the soundbite . . . and I can't compress what I have to say into a small enough soundbite to get it on T.V." . . . "The press is generally too lazy to research this subject for themselves and seems ready to accept whatever pap is fed to them by Cooperstown."

And as for Cooperstown, in Chapter 5 of this book you discovered how, in 1939, the National Baseball Hall of Fame came to be located in the small village of Cooperstown N.Y., a place where the Hall of Fame founders were lead to believe that baseball had been "invented" by a Civil War hero by the name of Abner Doubleday, one hundred years earlier.

Then, just before celebrations were to be held which

commemorated the combined opening of the Hall of Fame and baseball's so-called "centennial", they discovered that the Doubleday story was nothing but pure baloney . . . but they went ahead and held the festivities anyway.

"Now they could have stopped what they were doing, but they had decided that they were already in too deep financially . . . and publicity wise, it was good for baseball," says Speiser, who adds: "think of the irony of it all — this whole celebration was a fraud — so they have this guilty conscience at the Hall of Fame that has survived until today, where there's this terrible secret, this skeleton in their closet, that they don't want anybody to know about."

The reason for the Hall of Fame's reluctance to acknowledge the true origin of baseball also appears to be financial, they seem to think that the Doubleday myth helps to bring people (and dollars) into Cooperstown, and that, if the truth got out, attempts might even be made to move the Hall of Fame somewhere else!

When Stephen Speiser appeared with Hall of Fame president Ed Stack on a 1992 New Jersey cable television program which was broadcast state wide, Speiser says that Stack proclaimed that he "was concerned about what the impact of what we were doing might have on Cooperstown, as Cooperstown's primary industrial base is the Hall of Fame and the cottage industries that it spins off." Which brought Speiser to the conclusion that "whatever static that was coming out of Cooperstown was essentially because of the fact that they were concerned about the dollars that were flowing into the town."

Speiser feels that the Hall of Fame's paranoia is unjustified. "Cooperstown is so well established as part of the lore of baseball, that even if the reason for its location is incorrect, the fact that the Hall of Fame was sited there for the last 50 years or so, and everyone from Babe Ruth on, every great that's been inducted since 1936, has made the trek up to Cooperstown, it's become part of the lore and history of baseball." Speiser doesn't think that anybody

*Across the street from the coffee factory is a small park and playground called Elysian Park.*

would be in favor of moving the Hall of Fame, and that after 50 years they should be secure enough to publicly come clean on the Doubleday fable.

"What I had envisioned and hoped for was co-operation between Cooperstown and us," says Speiser, whose real goal is to set up a satellite museum at Elysian Fields which would get loaning exhibits from Cooperstown — something which would most likely end up helping to promote the Hall of Fame in Cooperstown, anyway, but the folks that run the Hall of Fame don't look at it that way. They seem to have this head-in-the-sand attitude that has existed ever since the place opened in 1939.

And why is getting the story of Alexander Cartwright and the Knickerbockers out to the world so important? "It was Alexander Cartwright's conception of the game that gave baseball it's meaning," says Speiser. "He changed the

*On a boulevard near the coffee factory, a Hoboken civic group erected this monument to Hoboken's baseball past.*

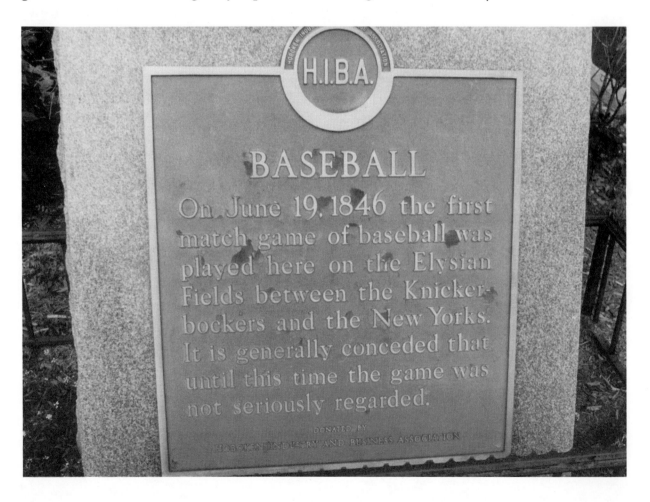

fundamental character of the game. The Knickerbocker club was the model; every other club that later evolved into the National Association of Baseball Players and the subsequent leagues that evolved from that, all came to Elysian Fields, and all saw the Knickerbockers play and then they brought it back to Brooklyn, and they brought it back to New York, and they brought it back to wherever they went . . . and they would write to the Knickerbocker club and ask for a copy of their rules. They got very excited by what they saw!" . . . "You could trace the history of baseball back 3000 years, if you like, but it all flows through Elysian Fields and the Knickerbocker Club. Alexander Cartwright and the Knickerbockers were the men responsible for giving us the game that we know as baseball, and they deserve a special place in history."

And what's next on his agenda? As of the publication of this book, Stephen Speiser is concentrating his efforts on helping the state of New Jersey to organize a gigantic baseball celebration to be held in Hoboken on June 19, 1996 in honor of the 150th anniversary of the birth of the game, for it was, after all, exactly a century and a half earlier, on June 19, 1846, that Alexander Cartwright and the Knickerbockers introduced baseball to the world at Elysian Fields.

And in conjunction with this, Speiser is lobbying the U.S. Congress to declare, in 1996, that June 19 would, from then on, be celebrated as a National Baseball Day. He has helped to write a resolution to this effect and has had both the U.S. Senators from New Jersey, as well as numerous State and local politicians, sign it. It will be presented to the U.S Congress at the appropriate time.

"There's no reason why there shouldn't be a National Baseball Day," says Speiser. "Baseball is a very important part of our culture — it's right up there with Mom and apple pie — and there is no more appropriate date for such a day than June 19."

Could it be that Alexander Cartwright will finally come to get the honor and recognition he deserves? Well, in his corner, he could have no better fighter for his cause than this New Jersey attorney.

And just why does he do it? "I'm an advocate, that's my profession, it's my role in life," says Speiser, who adds: "I can't think of a better cause to get behind than this."

# A CONVERSATION WITH
# ALEXANDER CARTWRIGHT IV

Alexander Cartwright IV is the great-great-grandson of the father of baseball. For all of his life he has known of the incredible baseball achievements and legacy of his long overlooked ancestor. He was born in Hawaii, grew up there and in Southern California (where he played Little League baseball as a lad) and later lived in Montana and Washington State. He is a computer analyst and now lives in the Seattle area with his wife and three children, where he operates his own firm which supplies accounting software to small businesses.

*Alexander Cartwright IV (left) poses with attorney Stephen Speiser (center) and former major leaguer Bobby Thompson at a recent Baseball Day celebration in Hoboken, N.J.*

*How Baseball Began*: When you played baseball as a boy, I guess there were times when you told the other kids that your great-great-grandfather invented the game. What was their reaction?

*Alexander Cartwright IV*: Well, you know back then nobody believed it . . . occasionally somebody would come across an article in the paper and they'd clip it out and so on, but the kids still wouldn't consider that to be something real, you had to show them something that was considered gospel like the *Colliers Encyclopedia* or the *Farmer's Almanac* or something like that, and then once they realized it was true they got pretty excited. I think people nowadays get more excited about it than they did when I was a kid.

*H.B.B.*: Do you think that the Hall of Fame in Cooperstown will ever come to their senses and give your great-great-grandfather the honor and recognition he deserves, and acknowledge the fact that, for all these years they have been honoring a man [Abner Doubleday] who had absolutely nothing to do with baseball?

A.C. IV: I don't know. This whole situation is apparently embarrassing to them. What they're probably going to do is come out and claim that there wasn't anybody that invented baseball, that it was kind of an evolutionary process.

*H.B.B.*: Well it was in a way, but it was nevertheless your great-great-grandfather who ultimately put all the various elements together and came up with the game that we now know as baseball. Have you ever been to Cooperstown?

A.C. IV: No, not yet, but I hope to go there sometime in the near future.

*H.B.B.*: Has anyone from the Hall of Fame ever contacted you in regards to your great-great-grandfather?

A.C. IV: No, not really. I did meet some people from the Hall of Fame a couple of years ago in Hoboken though, when I went there for the Baseball Day events. Actually, they were pretty nice to me, and said that I should let them know if I'm ever going to come out.

H.B.B.: I understand that the Hall of Fame has a number of your great-great-grandfather's artifacts and papers buried somewhere in their archives.

A.C. IV: Yes, the family gave quite a few artifacts to the Hall of Fame around the time of his induction in 1938. They probably have about 80 per cent of all artifacts of his that are related to the origins of baseball.

H.B.B.: But they don't have them on public display?

A.C. IV: Apparently not. I imagine if I went there and wanted to look at them, that they would let me do so.

H.B.B.: You just mentioned going out to Hoboken for the Baseball Day Events, where I understand, you were the guest of honor at a celebration that was basically designed to pay homage to your great-great-grandfather. When you arrived there, what was your first impression?

A.C IV: It was absolutely crazy. I had taken the Red Eye flight out of Seattle and didn't get into New York until 7:30 in the morning. Stephen Speiser picked me up at the airport, took me down to the ball field where a bunch of people stuck cameras in my face, and I began doing press conferences 45 minutes off the plane! But they take their baseball very seriously out there and it's fun to see that. I thought the celebrations were very interesting — I thought it was kind of neat that they actually went as far as they did to try and get recognition for the 19th of June and I gave them as much help as I possibly could, but you know, it's only as good as the public wants to honor it; if they lose interest in it, then what can you do? It's not important to them, and your efforts are counter-productive at that point, other than just to set the facts straight, and I think that Stephen Speiser did a good job of that. I hope that the result of all this will be that the people at Cooperstown will finally come to their senses and lay the Doubleday myth to rest.

*H.B.B.:* Previous to the time that Stephen Speiser first got in touch with you and invited you to come out to Hoboken, had other people discovered your great-great-grandfather's baseball achievements and contacted you about him?

A.C. IV: Well, this kind of thing happens about every 10 years. Before Stephen contacted me, the Hawaiian Islanders baseball club wanted me to come out to Honolulu and open up their baseball season by throwing the opening pitch, back in 1978. They were having a big, celebration to honor my great-great-grandfather not only as the father of baseball, but also because he was a great statesman in Honolulu. And then in 1968, a writer by the name of Harold Peterson contacted me in regards to a book he was doing on my great-great-grandfather [which ultimately turned out to be *The Man Who Invented Baseball*, the biography of Alexander Cartwright Jr.] . . . so about every 10 years or so my great-great-grandfather gets a lot of notoriety, and it goes on for a bit and then it dies away, and then someone else discovers him and it starts all over again.

*H.B.B.:* I certainly hope that the current interest in him is not just a passing thing . . . this is an incredible story. Your great-great-grandfather led an amazing life. It's hard to believe that he's gone virtually undiscovered for all these years — you'd think that someone would have made a movie about him by now!

A.C. IV: Oh, it is an incredible story, the fact that he virtually invented baseball when he was in New York and then, almost immediately, he left there and travelled by wagon train across the country in pre-Civil War days, enduring incredible hardships — this wasn't a nice quiet ride on Amtrak you know, he virtually walked all the way. Then when he got to California he actually found a bit of gold, and then he went on to Hawaii and became a great statesman over there . . . it sure would make a great movie.

*H.B.B.*: Are you now personally involved in anything that will help to get your great-great-grandfather the honor and recognition he deserves?

A.C. IV: I have just begun the task of petitioning the U.S. Post Office to issue a postage stamp in honor of my great-great-grandfather which would coincide with the forthcoming 150th anniversary of the birth of baseball in 1996.

*H.B.B.*: Speaking of '96, do you think that in that year, what with a major celebration planned for Hoboken, and the possibilities of both a National Baseball Day declared in your great-great-grandfather's honor and a postage stamp issued on his behalf as well, that the national media will finally pick up on his story and make him a household name?

A.C. IV: Well, it's like this: the story may pick up a lot of publicity, barring anything else in the baseball world that is of greater importance — like another strike for instance, or any major political story that's hot at the time. I mean, I think the press looks upon something like this as secondary or tertiary in nature. We'll just have to wait and see what happens.

*H.B.B*: Well, good luck with your postage stamp efforts, and with any kind of luck at all, maybe in a few years your great-great-grandfather will finally get the honor and recognition he deserves.

A.C. IV: I certainly hope so. It's long overdue . . . long overdue.

# BASEBALL MILESTONES
# OF THE 1800s

1846 - The Birth of Baseball — The first game between two organized teams played under Alexander Cartwright's rules and regulations takes place at Elysian Fields in Hoboken, New Jersey on June 19.

1854 - The weight of the ball is doubled from around 0 ounces to 0 ounces.

1857 - First convention of baseball clubs held in New York City. A rules committee is set up.

1858 - The National Association of Base Ball Players is formed to oversee the game and administrate the rules and regulations.

1864 - Fair balls caught on the first bounce were no longer considered an out.

1868 - Called strikes become part of the game.

1871 - The first professional baseball league, The National Association of Professional Base Ball Players, is formed.

   - The Dead Ball Era Begins — In order to help curb high game scores that sometimes exceeded a total of 100 runs in nine innings the amount of rubber used in the ball was restricted to one ounce.

1876 - The National League is formed. It replaces the National Association.

1878 - First gloves introduced — They were open fingered, worn on both hands, had very little padding and were originally intended for the protection of the hands. (Gloves specifically designed for fielding the ball did not come along until 1885.)

1879 - Walks first adopted. Nine balls got a batter to first base.

1881 - Pitching distance changed from 45 feet to 50 feet.

1883 - Pitchers allowed to throw overhand.

   - Foul balls caught on the first bounce were no longer considered an out.

1888 - Three strike rule adopted.

1889 - Four balls got a batter to first.

1891 - Substitution rule instituted. Previously substitutions were only allowed in the case of an injury or by permission of the other team.

1893 - Pitching distance changed to the present 60 feet 6 inches.

# EPILOGUE

## THE MAN WHO GAVE
## US BASEBALL

As was pointed out in chapter 6 of this book, they remember Alexander Cartwright in Hawaii, but unfortunately he is virtually unknown in the rest of the baseball world. This is due to a combination of factors:

- The fact that he disappeared from North America only a few years after virtually inventing the game.
- The fact that he was a very modest man; he did not brag about his baseball achievements.
- The fact that Al Spalding tried to re-write baseball history (and almost succeeded) by totally ignoring Cartwright and promoting the Doubleday story.
- The fact that the National Baseball Hall of Fame (which certainly should know better) has virtually ignored one of their own members (Cartwright) and instead has perpetuated the Doubleday myth for all of these years.
- The fact that Major League Baseball has consistently remained almost totally silent on the whole subject.

Now this is not some big plot against Alexander Cartwright, not some conscious conspiracy. No, it is, unfortunately, a combination of an ongoing series of events that has gone uncorrected for far too long.

It's time to turn this whole thing around. It's time that baseball recognized and *celebrated* its past — its *true* past! And *it can all be changed*!

It was approximately a century and a half ago that Alexander Cartwright gave us this great game of baseball, and it's time he was honored for it!

How can this be done? Well, the Hall of Fame can start things off by finally giving up on the Doubleday fable and letting the poor old General rest peacefully in his grave.

And Major League Baseball can certainly help, by publicly acknowledging the true history of the game and giving Alexander Cartwright, the true founder of baseball, all of the honor and recognition that he deserves.

These are some of the ways that Alexander Cartwright could, and should, be honored:

- There should be a statue of Alexander Cartwright erected at every baseball park in the land.
- A National Baseball Day should be celebrated each year in his honor (and it should be held on June 19, for it was on June 19, 1846 that the first game of baseball was played between two organized teams, under Cartwright's rules and regulations, at Elysian Fields in Hoboken New Jersey).
- Elysian Fields should be (at least partially) restored to its former glory and a monument (or museum) be erected there to honor Alexander Cartwright.
- Throughout the land there should be baseball leagues, baseball teams, and baseball stadiums named after Cartwright. (For example, how about renaming the Little League "the Alexander Cartwright League"? This would be a most appropriate way to honor the Father of Baseball, because Little League baseball is played the way it was in Alexander Cartwright's day — by amateurs playing for the sheer fun of it, the way Cartwright intended the game to be played!)
- The World Series trophy should be renamed the Cartwright trophy (or how about a Cartwright Cup?).
- The U.S. Postal Service should be urged to issue a postage stamp which would honor Alexander Cartwright.
- People everywhere need to form local organizations and societies to honor the early days of baseball. These groups would hold annual "Turn Back The Clock" or

"Old-Time" games where everyone dresses in old-style uniforms and plays baseball the way it was originally played.

- Major and Minor League Ball Clubs should be encouraged to hold Cartwright Days or Nights at their ballparks. The festivities would, of course, start off with an old-time baseball game to be played before the regular game.

- *You* can campaign for Cartwright by contacting your favorite baseball writers, columnists and broadcasters, as well as the editors of the sports sections of your local newspapers and those of national baseball magazines, and tell them that it's about time they did a story on Alexander Cartwright and the true origin of baseball!

- *You* can encourage both the National Baseball Hall of Fame and Major League Baseball to change their ways and finally give Alexander Cartwright and the Knickerbockers the proper honor and recognition they deserve. An appropriate way to do this would be to send off a letter or fax to both of these institutions:

THEIR ADDRESSES ARE:

National Baseball Hall of Fame
P.O. Box 590
Cooperstown, NY 13326
Fax - (607) 547-2044

Major League Baseball
350 Park Ave.
New York, NY 10022
Fax - (212) 355-0007

# IN CONCLUSION...

It's time for baseball to honor, celebrate and promote its true early history, for it's a great history. Not only should Alexander Cartwright be honored, but all of the other great early pioneers of the game deserve recognition as well — men who, throughout the early years, experimented with the rules and helped to refine the game . . . men such as those who played for the New York Knickerbockers and all the other early clubs in the 1840s, '50s and '60s . . . and those innovators who were part of the early professional game in the 1870s, '80s and '90s, men whose names every true baseball aficionado should know by heart: Harry Wright, William Hulbert, "Old Hoss" Radburn, "Cap" Anson, "King" Kelly, Chris Von der Ahe, Al Spalding, Henry Chadwick, Charles Commiskey, Ban Johnson and Wee Willie "Hit it where they ain't" Keeler, to name just a few.

Yes, they all deserve to be honored (even that rascal Spalding), and you can start by glorifying the man who virtually started it all, and without whom there probably wouldn't even be baseball today — Alexander Cartwright Jr., the 25-year-old intuitive genius from New York City, who turned a simple children's game into a game that adults could play. He was truly the man who gave us baseball.

# PHOTO CREDITS

All photos courtesy of:
National Baseball Library, Cooperstown, N.Y.
with the exception of the following:

New York Public Library - Pages 24, 47, 53, 59 & 60.

Hawaii State Archives - Pages 116 & 119.

Stephen Speiser - Page 132.

The author - Pages 125, 126, 128, 130.

Original artwork on pages 5, 6, 16 & 119
by Pam Staples.

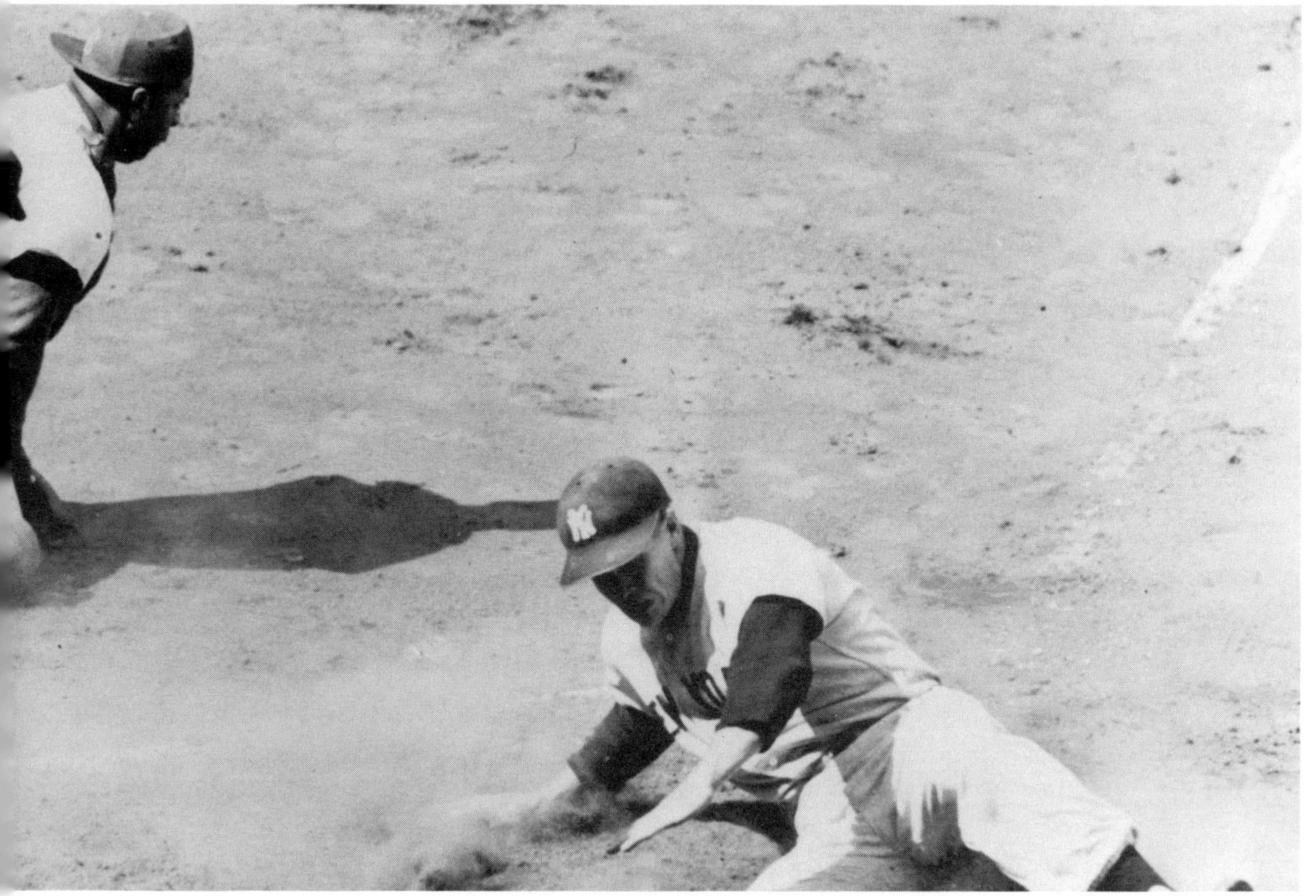